T0049338

All Tangled Up in Autism and Chronic Illness

of related interest

So, I'm Autistic
An Introduction to Autism for Young Adults and Late Teens
Sarah O'Brien
ISBN 978 1 83997 226 3
eISBN 978 1 83997 227 0

The Autism-Friendly Cookbook
Lydia Wilkins
Illustrated by Emily of @21andsensory
ISBN 978 1 83997 082 5
eISBN 978 1 83997 083 2

Taking Off the Mask
Practical Exercises to Help Understand and Minimise
the Effects of Autistic Camouflaging
Hannah Louise Belcher
Foreword by Will Mandy, PHD, DClinPsy
ISBN 978 1 78775 589 5
eISBN 978 1 78775 590 1

Queerly Autistic
The Ultimate Guide for LGBTQIA+ Teens on the Spectrum
Erin Ekins
ISBN 978 1 78775 171 2
eISBN 978 1 78775 172 9

All Tangled Up in Autism and Chronic Illness

A GUIDE TO NAVIGATING MULTIPLE CONDITIONS

CHARLI CLEMENT

Jessica Kingsley Publishers
London and Philadelphia

First published in Great Britain in 2024 by Jessica Kingsley Publishers
An imprint of John Murray Press

1

Copyright © Charli Clement 2024

The right of Charli Clement to be identified as the Author of the Work has been
asserted by them in accordance with the Copyright, Designs and Patents Act 1988.

All rights reserved. No part of this publication may be reproduced, stored
in a retrieval system, or transmitted, in any form or by any means without
the prior written permission of the publisher, nor be otherwise circulated
in any form of binding or cover other than that in which it is published and
without a similar condition being imposed on the subsequent purchaser.

*The information contained in this book is not intended to replace the services
of trained medical professionals or to be a substitute for medical advice. You
are advised to consult a doctor on any matters relating to your health, and in
particular on any matters that may require diagnosis or medical attention.*

A CIP catalogue record for this title is available from the
British Library and the Library of Congress

ISBN 978 1 83997 524 0
eISBN 978 1 83997 525 7

Printed and bound in Great Britain by TJ Books Ltd

Jessica Kingsley Publishers' policy is to use papers that are natural,
renewable and recyclable products and made from wood grown in
sustainable forests. The logging and manufacturing processes are expected
to conform to the environmental regulations of the country of origin.

Jessica Kingsley Publishers
Carmelite House
50 Victoria Embankment
London EC4Y 0DZ

www.jkp.com

John Murray Press
Part of Hodder & Stoughton Ltd
An Hachette Company

MIX
Paper from
responsible sources
FSC® C013056
FSC
www.fsc.org

For Mum – for every appointment, phone call and moment of advocacy for me in the last 13 years.

&

In memory of Simran – I hope I'm making you proud.

Contents

Acknowledgements

The eight-year-old Charli with a maxed out library card and the 13-year-old book blogger with a dream would never have believed I got a book deal at 21 (though they'd probably be more shocked to learn they're autistic and chronically ill). It wouldn't have been possible without all of the incredible people I have in my life.

Thank you to Lynda and the team at JKP for believing in me and trusting me with this book – the support throughout has meant the world, especially to have someone that believed in me when I didn't, and who put up with all the panicked Zoom calls.

Thank you to my family – for being there for me, allowing me to talk about the book all the time, pushing me when I complained that I couldn't do it, and for being my rock throughout every part of my long journey with my health and neurodivergence. That last part goes especially to Tyler, Eleni and Connor, who have always taken everything in their stride even at their young ages.

To Gabbi, Fi, Jaimee, all my wonderful friends, and my second family at the 32nd, who have had to hear every rant, every time I've thought I can't do it, every infodump and every lament that I couldn't think of a title (we got there eventually).

To Leanne Maskell, because this book wouldn't even have happened without her and I'd still be stuck and lost at the 15,000 word mark, and Ellie Middleton for being the best cheerleader.

Thank you to my teachers throughout school and those at university who did everything they could to support me, and to the good professionals I've seen along the way – especially in the last two years.

To all the chronically ill and autistic people I had the pleasure and honour to interview throughout this book, with all their unique perspectives. It wouldn't be the same book without them, and it is a thousand times richer because of them.

To the disabled, autistic and chronically ill communities online and beyond, who saved my life, taught me so much, and watched me grow up as I learnt who I am over the last decade.

And finally, to you. I hope this book can give you something you need.

Introduction

Every time I have received a diagnosis, I've been handed a shiny, printed leaflet, splashed with 'living with [insert condition here]'. They detail common symptoms or traits, support available (which is often not much), and try to explain how I will experience that condition.

Except, for me, those leaflets have never reflected my own experience, and for a long time I couldn't figure out why.

Eventually, I figured it out. As someone who is autistic, as well as being dyspraxic and having ADHD, I experience many of my chronic illness symptoms subtly differently, whether that be in how they affect my sensory needs, or in dealing with interoception issues. The way I manage some of my autistic traits is also affected by my chronic illness and the way I can't do certain things that others can.

Getting a handle on my chronic illnesses has always been impacted by being autistic. I struggle to explain and process my pain, meaning doctors often haven't believed me, and physio or testing is more difficult to participate in. My relationships and education have been intertwined with these struggles, my sensory needs, and more.

I've never felt like there is enough information out there about how being autistic and chronically ill can clash or combine, and how this needs to be understood within different sectors, from healthcare to education – and there certainly isn't enough information for individuals to understand it for themselves. That's the gap I hope to begin to fill with this book.

As well as the experience of being both autistic and chronically ill often seeming like a bit of a paradox, it's also a much more common experience than many believe. More research is being done on this, such as that which recently showed that hypermobility, chronic pain and dysautonomia are more common in autistic people (as well as those with ADHD or Tourette's) than in the general population.[1]

This book won't cover every experience a chronically ill and autistic person has. Autism is a spectrum and every chronic illness affects people differently even when they have the same condition. However, I hope it can begin to help you unpick and understand the ways autism and chronic illness can interact, and how to support different needs.

Where did my story begin?

I was ten when we first spotted some problems with my mobility – pain when I walked, and my knees turning the wrong way stopping me from standing with my legs together. I was confused, because I thought everyone had pain when they walked, even though mine hurt after only very short distances.

I was pushed from doctor to doctor in different hospital departments, trying physiotherapy, MRIs, and countless blood tests, but it wasn't until I was 17 that I received a proper diagnosis of hypermobility spectrum disorder from a specialist rheumatologist after my health significantly deteriorated. Knowledge of my postural orthostatic tachycardia syndrome (POTS) took another year after that.

I originally had doctors tell me I was fine because I still attended school, and endless others assumed it was all in my head. Now, I know so much more about my conditions, how they present differently and that it truly was never just in my head.

Unlike the slow, demoralising process that became my journey to eventual chronic illness diagnoses, the discovery I was autistic was instead sudden, almost out of nowhere.

I started having panic attacks when I was 14, first seemingly situational and not too worrying. A few weeks later, it became evident that they were going to stick around, and were happening up to twice a day at one point.

Ironically, it was a doctor we saw for my chronic pain that spotted it first. He saw that I had walked on my toes since I was three years old – which we, of course, had no idea was an autistic trait – and that I was about to be referred to CAMHS (Child and Adolescent Mental Health Services). He turned around and directly asked if I was autistic, and we had never thought about it.

That doctor infantilised me through that appointment. It was clear that he had decided I was autistic but didn't know how to treat autistic people and saw us all in a stereotypical way. We never saw him again after that because of this, but, after a lot of research and digging deep into our internalised ableism, we went into my first CAMHS appointment knowing far more about me than we had a few months before.

And so, this was one of the times that my journey as a chronically ill person and as an autistic person visibly, notably collided – but there is far more to it than that.

Being autistic and chronically ill is intrinsic to my identity and to how I live my life. There is nothing wrong with your disabilities being a huge part of you, even though society tells us we should ignore them and keep going.

My disabilities have changed how I access every part of my life, how I find my communities and navigate my social life and family, and more besides. Why wouldn't that define me?

Who is this book for?

This book will discuss many experiences of being autistic and chronically ill, with anecdotes from individuals with a variety of chronic illnesses and unique perspectives. Please note pseudonyms have been used for some interviewees when requested.

Some of them will be 'self-diagnosed' as autistic and/or with their chronic illness, i.e. they have not received a formal diagnosis from a doctor. Self-diagnosis is seen as valid within the autistic and disabled communities due to the barriers that marginalised people may face whilst seeking a professional diagnosis, ranging from the financial privilege to seek out a private diagnosis, to racial or gender-based privilege (as white, cisgendered men are less likely to struggle to get a diagnosis), which we will discuss in more detail later in the book.

Whether you are chronically ill and/or autistic yourself or not, this book should shine a light on the support we need, and the difficulties we face.

Much of this book will be addressed to a reader who is chronically ill and autistic themselves, but you can also read this if you are someone who is trying to understand better, whether that be as a healthcare professional, a family member or a friend. There are some sections including advice specifically for these individuals, too.

A note on language

This book will use identity-first language (for example, autistic person or disabled person) unless someone quoted has specified a preference for other terms.

Much of the autistic and disabled communities prefer identity-first language over person-first language (for example, person with autism) because we believe that our disabilities cannot be separated from the rest of us. By saying we are 'with' them, it can imply they are not a true part of us or that we shouldn't want it to be a big part of our identities.

'Non-disabled' will also be used instead of 'able-bodied' to refer to those who are not disabled. This is because 'able-bodied' can imply that those who are disabled in a non-physical way, for example in being neurodivergent or mentally ill, are a part of a group that doesn't experience ableism.

'Allistic' will be used to specifically refer to those who are not autistic. 'Neurotypical' instead means those who are not neurodivergent, and being neurodivergent refers not only to autism but to many other conditions, including but not limited to ADHD, dyspraxia, dyslexia, Tourette's syndrome and epilepsy.

An introduction to models of disability

Throughout this book, I will be referring to autism and chronic illnesses as disabilities. This will primarily be based within the idea of the social model of disability.

The social model of disability says that disabled people are such due to society's lack of accommodations and accessibility, rather than the condition itself.

The social model is used instead of the medical model, which says that disabled people are impaired by their conditions or 'impairments'. Many of us don't believe our disabilities are impairments, and a lot of the problems we do face are a product of society.

The social model is not perfect. Many autistic people discuss that even if society removed many of its barriers to autistic people, like making better sensory environments and making communication more accessible, they would still be disabled by some of their internal traits. However, others would then argue that within the social model you would be given the support, space and rest to contend with this, rather than being forced into working within society. It is an ongoing model, but is one of the most effective currently.

There are other models that do not centre the idea of impairment the way the medical model does. Another is the human rights model of disability, which says that being disabled should not undermine a person's dignity or human rights.

How to use this book

There isn't a singular way to read or use this book. Everyone will get different things from it, and you might find some sections more helpful than others.

You might prefer to dip in and out of the book as and when you come up against a problem or when you are looking for advice about something specific. Or you might prefer to read through it in order to look at all the different topics in it. It's up to you!

If you are a healthcare professional or a teacher reading this book, you might find the following chapters most useful: Chapter 1, Navigating diagnosis and healthcare; Chapter 3, Sensory needs;

Chapter 5, Education and employment; and Chapter 8, Gender, medical misogyny and menstrual health. At the end of each chapter there are some key takeaways that I think are some of the biggest points of each chapter, but you might want to add your own to them or reflect on what you have learnt.

1

Navigating diagnosis and healthcare

Being chronically ill can mean a long journey towards getting appropriate medical support or a diagnosis. It can include tracking down the right specialists, identifying the issues through your symptoms and testing, and then trying to work out what support you need after that. Adding being autistic can make this process even more complicated.

After ten years of being pushed from department to department and doctor to doctor, I am pretty well seasoned in navigating the many issues that healthcare can cause autistic and chronically ill people, including the effect on my own emotions and feelings, difficulty communicating with professionals and trying to navigate the many tests and kinds of care. It often isn't easy, but there are definitely things we can do to cushion the difficulties we have within the system.

This chapter will explore some of the first steps towards diagnosis and support, how you can put measures in place to try and make this more effective and comfortable for you, and how autism and chronic illness intertwine when accessing healthcare for either one of them.

Communication

'Communication difficulties' are often touted as one of the key parts of autism. Many of us would argue they aren't difficulties, we just communicate differently to allistic people. We often prefer directness, which is seen as rude or blunt. Some autistic people are non-speaking. This doesn't mean a lack of communication – society sees talking as one of the only valid forms of communication due to normalisation, but non-speaking people can use many other forms that are just as valid.

But the way that society has decided autistic people cannot communicate has a significant impact on a lot of areas of our life, and for chronically ill autistic people this can combine particularly within our healthcare.

For many of us, being autistic and chronically ill can often mean we have experienced trauma, whether that be away from healthcare or within trying to access it. This can add an additional barrier when we are trying to establish good relationships in healthcare and interact with professionals, and this is something they should consider.

Talking to healthcare professionals

Even at the age of 22, I still take my mum to most of my appointments with doctors. I find it useful to have the back-up, but once upon a time it wasn't just that – I simply couldn't talk to the doctors by myself. I could say a few sentences here and there, but I needed her to discuss my history, explain my symptoms.

There's nothing wrong with needing to take someone with you to appointments. You are within your rights to have someone with you, whether that is a parent, a personal assistant or carer, or an independent advocate.

This may not be just for the reason of needing someone to physically talk to the doctor. Even in times that I found myself more confident than normal to do so, having someone with me helped me to process and understand the questions I was being asked. It also helped me remember things I couldn't, because I often forget how long I've experienced a symptom, or can't put something into wider context. After the appointment, it would mean I could discuss what happened and make sure I had interpreted it all correctly.

I also struggle to describe my pain, which my advocate can support me to think about. This is due to interoception issues, which you can read more about in the next section of this chapter.

It also helps with accountability. There are doctors who are less likely to put us forward for testing or further referrals, instead just discharging us and closing our file. This might be because they don't understand what is going on, because they don't have the knowledge to untangle your different traits or symptoms, or because they haven't tried to understand how you are communicating your needs. Having someone there doesn't necessarily stop them from doing that, but it does mean that someone has witnessed their behaviour, can vocalise disagreement, and push forward in a way that you might not feel confident or able to.

JJ is an autistic and chronically ill person who has Ehlers-Danlos syndrome (EDS) as well as a heart condition, gastroparesis and other physical and mental health conditions. They described struggling with eye contact when speaking to professionals:

> Because of my autism, I don't like eye contact. It makes me uncomfortable and feels far too intimate, and I can't concentrate on the words a person is saying if I'm trying to figure out the socially acceptable amount of time to be looking

at a person's face. A lot of healthcare professionals have accused me of lying or not listening to them because I don't look at their eyes when they talk to me or I talk to them. This feels very unfair. – **JJ**

Some autistic people find it helpful to set out things that they struggle with at the start of an appointment in the hope to prevent such accusations as this. Whilst not foolproof, some find that doctors are more open when they know this. You could use a communication card or pre-written letter to hand to them if you don't want to explain it verbally.

Neve is an autistic person who has polycystic ovary syndrome (PCOS), pre-menstrual dysphoric disorder and non-24-hour sleep wake disorder. She talked about not having to repeat things:

You need to overcompensate for lack of knowledge and experience. Write down every detail about your condition as if they don't know about it – chances are, they don't. This goes especially for poorly understood and rarer conditions.

Repeating yourself is exhausting so I guess keeping a one-size-fits-all cheat sheet to hand over can help save writing out the same thing every time. For example, I have odontophobia and I bring the same notes to remind my dentist of what I need every time. I'd say have someone with you to advocate for you as well since the explaining really does drain me quite quickly and I can often feel like I'm on the defensive, or not being believed. – **Neve**

An issue many of us can encounter whilst navigating healthcare and talking to professionals is the way our symptoms and traits often have crossovers or will wrongly be attributed to something we are already diagnosed with. For example, some people find their chronic fatigue is seen as part of their executive functioning differences. It can be difficult to navigate this because sometimes this may actually be the case, but often it isn't properly explored. It can help to make symptom logs that show patterns, ask for additional testing or make a diary of how any medication has changed different symptoms or traits. You can also consider putting in reasonable adjustments or accommodations for yourself as if you already had a different diagnosis, and see if this has any impact or not.

Being patronised

An issue that many autistic people come up against is infantilisation – being treated as if they are a child just because they are autistic. This can often result in being patronised by healthcare professionals who give you the impression that they don't believe that you can understand your own symptoms, traits or conditions.

This is unfortunately often twofold for chronically ill autistic people, because chronic illnesses are often left undiagnosed and not believed for far too long. Chronically ill people are told it's all in their head, that they couldn't possibly be that unwell. Studies show that patients with multiple or worsening symptoms are often labelled as 'difficult' by physicians, causing worse outcomes or them being discharged.[1] This includes many with EDS – which commonly co-occurs alongside autism – who can spend years in the 'diagnostic odyssey' of tests, procedures, wrong diagnoses and more.[2]

Many people wait years to be taken seriously – for example, endometriosis takes an average of eight years to be diagnosed in the UK.[3]

This is particularly seen by those who are misogyny affected, which we will explore further in Chapter 8. In a Danish study of nearly 7 million patients, it was found that on average women received diagnoses for conditions like diabetes 4.5 years later than men.[4]

It is also evident that Black chronically ill people and chronically ill people of the global majority are particularly affected – for example, being less likely than white patients to receive pain medications, and receiving less medication.[5]

When you add being autistic, it is assumed that you are just misunderstanding something.

Many chronically ill people who have found ways to get through their day-to-day lives, such as finding ways to manage education, work or social situations, can have that used as evidence as to why we can't be chronically ill or aren't having the symptoms to the extent we say we are.

It's also not uncommon for autistic people particularly to want to build up lots of knowledge around what they are experiencing, due to the development of special interests or our sense of rigour and justice, wanting to know everything about a topic. Although this is a well-documented phenomenon, many doctors take this as suspicious and think that we are reporting symptoms or traits just because we know they are related to the condition rather than because they are actively present. This can lead to us treading a thin line when it comes to our communication with healthcare professionals, not knowing what to say or what to hold back.

It's very important that doctors don't diminish patients, and are very careful not to dismiss concerns from autistic individuals about their potential conditions. Communication should be directed at the patient themselves and not just at an advocate, as this can be significantly patronising.

The bringing of an advocate should not mean that they are spoken to *instead* of you – they should be spoken to *alongside* you. They are support, not a replacement.

Using alternative communication

You should not feel ashamed if you struggle to speak to healthcare professionals, whether that be due to anxiety, struggling to get your thoughts together or any other reason. There is also no shame in being a non-speaking or partially speaking autistic person.

There is nothing wrong with needing to use other methods of communication instead of directly speaking during medical appointments.

This could be through a variety of methods. You may prefer to take someone with you such as an advocate, parent or carer as previously discussed in this chapter, though you may not feel that this gives you as much autonomy as you'd like.

It should be seen as completely acceptable for you to write down what you want to communicate, use Augmentative and Alternative Communication (AAC) such as picture boards or computer systems, or use communication cards. Communication cards can be bought online or made yourself, with a range of personalised phrases to show as needed.

Eli is an autistic 26-year-old with ADHD, hypermobility and idiopathic intracranial hypertension. He is also semi-speaking and an AAC user.

I'm semi-speaking and an AAC user. I've found that my physical health can really impact on my ability to use mouth-words. Low energy means that I have less capacity to speak, but using AAC has made it far easier to be heard.

I get really frustrated though, as people don't give me enough time to type a response. I've had to learn to be more persistent and assertive to be heard, especially with professionals and in the workplace. I've yet to find a comfortable solution for being able to communicate with my device whilst also using my rollator. At the moment, I have to sit down to type a response. I've found some success with picture communication cards, but there is only so much you can express with them.

Having a good communication partner is important. My best friend gives me the time and space to formulate a response. She encourages me to use AAC when she can see that I'm struggling with speech. She helps me advocate for myself with others. I appreciate it a lot. I've found that the combination of chronic illness, mobility difficulties, being autistic and being semi-speaking has led to a lot of infantilisation. People talk to me like I am a small child and don't think I am capable. They talk past me and speak to the people I am with instead. I often feel like I don't have much power and autonomy in my life. It isn't fair.

I've used AAC when I've been in the hospital. If I am in pain and distress, speech is impossible. It's important to make sure I have accurate health information pre-written in my AAC, so I don't have to try to type and explain things when I'm already overloaded. – **Eli**

Getting appointments and seeing specialists
You may find that you have difficulties communicating with hospitals and healthcare professionals before you even get in front of them.

This can be for a few different reasons. Some will be insistent that they can only take phone calls, where you might struggle with those as many autistic people often do. Due to rules around reasonable adjustments and access to services, services need to support you to contact them by email or text (for example).

You might need to reschedule an appointment or need to ask for more information before your first appointment. The former can be difficult if you struggle to communicate by phone – you could ask someone else to support you with this or use a text relay service if this isn't possible.

Asking for more information about an appointment, such as which doctor you are seeing or how a test will go, is perfectly acceptable. You might want to find out if you need to take anything with you, wear something specific, or about the rules around taking someone with you. This is something you shouldn't feel scared to do.

If you are struggling to get in contact with services, particularly if you struggle with phone calls and need another way to contact such as emailing but this is not provided, there are a few ways you could try to get support with this. You could return to your primary care doctor for more support, or use an advocate linked to the service for support. If this continues to not occur, you can then raise a more formal complaint via services such as PALS in the UK, or the relevant complaints department for patients.

Jasper is a profoundly deaf, autistic wheelchair user who has several conditions including EDS, POTS and myalgic encephalomyelitis (ME). He has difficulties talking to healthcare professionals due to having multiple disabilities that affect communication, but needs to regularly see a variety of professionals. He said:

Despite there already being legal obligations for the National Health Service in the UK like the Accessible Information

Standard and the Equality Act, [most people] haven't been trained on what they're supposed to be doing.

I think the biggest challenge is that my disabilities are very complex – I see many different consultants for different symptoms, like the chronic fatigue service, cardiology, gastroenterology and audiology. A person without my conditions might just go for a health check-up and see one consultant. They'd get the hospital letter and might need to change it or rearrange it once if the time clashes but that's the end, whereas for me it's more complicated. Due to ME I can't attend appointments before 10am or I'd be in so much pain I couldn't get home. And my personal assistant has to call them up when we get the letter to check the location is wheelchair accessible because despite it being on my records for seven years, we still have situations like being booked for a mobile MRI that's up two flights of stairs.

I also need an interpreter arranged for all of my appointments. This is often not arranged until the last minute so some appointments are constantly rescheduled. I was meant to see a dietician in November and I'm still waiting because they have to change [the appointment dates] every two weeks when they have waited until the day before to book an interpreter. It means I have to wait three plus months for a follow-up.

So because of all of this, as an autistic person there is a lot of change and stress, with last minute cancellations and making sure my PAs are available – and that's before I even get to the hospital. By the time I get there I'm already stressed and anxious that something else will go wrong. – **Jasper**

Interoception

Most people are only aware of five of our senses (touch, taste, smell, hearing and sight), but we actually have a few more, including proprioception (our ability to understand where our body is in space) and interoception (our ability to understand what is going on with our body). These additional senses are ones which are likely to particularly impact autistic and otherwise neurodivergent people, with us being under- or over-sensitive to them.

Interoception can cause you to be under- or over-aware of:

- being hungry or thirsty
- needing the toilet
- understanding how hot or cold you are
- sensitivity to pain
- being able to regulate your emotions
- feeling sensations in your body such as heart rate.

Symptoms of your chronic illness could fit within one or more of these sensations, such as having an irregular heart rate, having temperature regulation issues or losing your appetite. Therefore, if you struggle with interoception issues, you might find it more difficult to process, understand or discuss your symptoms.

Doctors often ask us to make diaries or logs of our symptoms in order for them to understand patterns or changes. This might be more difficult for autistic people for a variety of reasons, whether it be because they cannot describe or recognise these symptoms, or because they struggle to differentiate between feelings. Many of us often find that we cannot locate a pain within a specific part of the body, or cannot describe *how* it feels.

You may prefer to use a symptom app for these logs, rather than trying to write down your feelings on a blank piece of paper which puts more onus on you to find the words.

If you have to take medications or need to drink more water, you might find apps or alarms helpful for this too, as this means you don't have to rely on bodily sensations to prompt these actions.

Something I particularly struggle with as a chronically ill autistic person due to interoception differences when communicating with healthcare professionals is number scales. Many doctors like to bring them out so they can understand where your pain (or another symptom) is, or where you perceive it is.

To me, however, these are entirely abstract. My 7 is probably another person's 15, because I'm constantly in some level of chronic pain. How will they use this number to actually decide my healthcare? It confuses me and I find this very stressful.

Between not being able to talk about how the pain feels and not knowing how to put a pin on a scale, this can sometimes cause issues for healthcare professionals.

Instead, I try to tell them in advance that I might struggle with this, and we try to find other ways of understanding it.

I will tell them that it's better or worse than my average day, try and localise it to a specific area instead of my classic answer of 'everything', and try and work out if it's a pain I've ever had before or if it's something unique or new that might be worrying. I try to describe the pain in any way I can.

Remember: it's part of your doctor's job to work out what you're trying to say to them. They have to find alternative ways of understanding your physical symptoms as well as making reasonable adjustments for you as a neurodivergent patient.

Amber is a 21-year-old autistic and chronically ill disabled person. They have only more recently realised that they are autistic, and told me about how this was affected by both interoception differences and the focus on their chronic health issues:

Autism is something we came to think about a couple of years after I became chronically ill. With a little bit of hindsight, I think it went unrecognised in the early illness years because I wasn't experiencing enough of 'normal' day-to-day life to really understand the root underneath some of the difficulties I was experiencing. As some symptoms of my conditions can mirror autistic traits it was often put down to that. It is only now that things are a little bit more stable health wise, we have begun to be able to draw distinctions between the two but also acknowledge what traits predate chronic illness but were made more obvious by its onset.

They are interlinked extensively and having more knowledge about both aspects has helped me to a) understand my own body and b) explain things to other people, including medical professionals. For example, I always found explaining the sensation of different pains to professionals hard because all I could say was this really hurts. I couldn't differentiate whether it was a 'burning', ' pulling', 'stabbing' pain even when professionals asked multiple times. Now I can say, I'm autistic and this means I can struggle to describe body sensations, including pain – which is very well known to present differently for autistic folk. – **Amber**

Healthcare appointments for 'everyday' issues

Obviously, as chronically ill autistic people, we not only have healthcare appointments for our conditions – we can still get the flu, tonsillitis, sprain our ankles or any number of things… and actually in some cases we are more likely to experience these things.

Appointments and particularly testing for these sorts of 'every-day' health needs – rather than our chronic health needs or dis-abilities – can feel difficult and intrusive, particularly because we are already feeling run down at this point. The sensory aspect of having your throat looked at or your stomach touched can be extremely problematic, and it can be very difficult to answer questions about symptoms when said symptoms match up to your everyday experiences – when I'm asked if I'm struggling with fatigue, it feels like a silly question!

There is no single way to navigate these sorts of appointments. I often make my doctor aware of my sensory and communica-tion needs if they are not someone who has seen me before, and ask them for testing to be as quick and non-invasive as possible. I personally like to take someone with me where I can to aid this, but this is very much a personal preference not shared by every autistic and chronically ill person.

Many people may avoid going to the doctor for these sorts of issues until absolutely necessary. This is understandable but is not always safe, so you should make sure that if enough time passes or symptoms are severe enough that you still attend.

It can also be hard to know when something is bad enough as a chronically ill autistic person, because of the combination of your usual symptoms fluctuating and our common nature of being hyposensitive to interoception, meaning we don't realise we are ill. Symptom tracking apps can be useful here to work out what is new or a pattern.

Getting vaccinated
Vaccinations are another aspect of healthcare that can be more difficult for us to navigate as they can be very anxiety-causing and for some cause sensory discomfort; they can also mean our chronic symptoms are exacerbated for a few days depending on

how our immune systems respond. Saying that, however, they are an extremely important part of helping your body cope with infection, which is crucial for those of us who are immunosuppressed or get ill much more easily than our non-chronically ill peers.

Some of the ways getting vaccinated can be made easier by you or by healthcare professionals include:

- Booking a longer/double appointment to make sure you are comfortable before being vaccinated.
- Talking the process through with you.
- Allowing you to see the needle beforehand (this makes me feel worse, but for some people it can make the process more visible and clear).
- Having stim toys and sensory aids with you during the appointment. It may be better if the professional doesn't talk to you much, or it might help for them to distract you.
- Asking for appointment times at quieter times of the day.
- Having vaccines done at a place which feels best for you. In the case of more recent vaccines, there are many big centres, but this might feel much worse than your local doctors.
- Wearing clothing that doesn't cover the arms so you don't have to remove or move it.

Understanding and accepting your diagnosis

For many chronically ill and autistic people – whether you are both or just one – a diagnosis often doesn't arrive easily or quickly. It might come after years of fighting, or not understanding yourself, or at a crisis point. That can make understanding, accepting and untangling a diagnosis very difficult.

I am Black mixed race and I've often found that it has led to me feeling like an outcast in autistic spaces, which can be fairly White dominated. A lot of the assumptions that professionals make about my medical and cultural needs are based off what they know about White autistic and chronically ill people.

I've also found that I have difficulty being heard within my own family. There can often be high amount of (often warranted) suspicion towards the medical system in the Black community. Things tend to be resolved within the family. There have been times when my diagnosis has been disregarded and my needs have been back seated in favour of family values. – **Eli**

It should be reiterated at this point that self-diagnosis is generally accepted within the disabled, chronically ill and autistic communities due to the privilege-related barriers that can often play into receiving a diagnosis – such as the difficulties that those assigned female at birth or from racial and ethnic minorities are more likely to face. We will discuss this in more depth in Chapter 8, but this part of the chapter can still apply to learning about yourself when you are waiting to be diagnosed or have self-diagnosed.

Finding out you have a condition can change your outlook on your life, as you begin to understand why you experience certain things or why your personality is what it is.

That can come with a huge range of emotions, from grief, to bitterness and anger, all the way to relief and happiness. It can be a rollercoaster. These emotions might be directed at yourself, your family, your doctors.

Many might not know that being disabled requires us to be self-sustained and rely on ourselves most of the time ([more] than we deserve). Especially with autism or any neurodivergent conditions that don't have a lot of reliable resources from experts, it feels like we are bound to self-teach. Trials and errors and failures are always in our day-to-day experiences. – MS

You should let yourself feel all of this. Give yourself lots of time to process each emotion, and do not feel silly for feeling any of them.

You might find something like journaling helpful for this journey, such as through writing down your feelings, drawing them out, thinking about your past and unpicking different parts of yourself.

Aside from processing your emotions, you may need to do some learning on a more practical level. Your doctors might have given you some leaflets, or maybe offered a support group to attend. However, depending on the condition this might not be enough, or the latter might be difficult for you as an autistic individual if you struggle with anxiety or find it challenging to access new social situations, for example.

Particularly when discovering your identity, you often long for community. There is a huge community of autistic and chronically ill people available on social media that I always recommend people learn from – there's a list of people you should be following at the back of this book. Learn from people like you, rather than learning from what society says about our conditions.

In these spaces, you are more likely to find solutions to some of the things you might struggle with that are a bit more unconventional. However, you should make sure to use social media safely too, by using functions such as muting, blocking or reporting if you find something upsetting or damaging, and don't use any solutions or alternative treatments or supports that could be dangerous to you.

Medication

Medication tends to be part and parcel of any chronic illness, whether it be something to try and help your symptoms like pain or sleep disturbances, or as direct treatment of the illness itself.

Finding the right medication and dosage can be a difficult process for a variety of reasons, whether that is due to side effects, fear or how long it can take to find something that truly works.

> I believe my sensory difficulties mean I experience my symptoms differently and more intensively than other Crohn's patients. Pain management can also be difficult for me as I do not seem to react to pain medication in the same ways as other patients and do not get as much relief. – **Becky**

Finding the right medication

Your doctors should work with you to try and find medications that help you – lacking in side effects as far as possible whilst still doing what they are supposed to.

You might struggle to work out when the medication is doing its job if you are not sure what to look for, and if you have difficulties with your interoception and sensitivities to pain or emotion this may be a further issue.

However, there are ways to try and track this and communicate the changes (or lack thereof) to your team.

There are many apps which allow you to track your symptoms, or you could do this on paper too – you should pick something that works for you. Sometimes scales from 1–10 may be helpful as you can directly compare each day, but if this is too abstract, others will let you describe it or write down anything that helps you to remember how it feels. You should particularly note any big changes to what you are used to, whether positive or negative.

If you struggle to check in with yourself and focus on each of your pains or symptoms, there are exercises which might help you to do this.

For example, you could try a body scan: This can be done by your-self, but there are also many recordings out there to help you with the process so you only need to focus on the actions instead of worrying what you need to do next.

You should lie down or get comfortable before checking in on each part of your body from head to toes. When thinking about each part of you, you should try and notice if there is any pain, discomfort or ache. You might not know why, or exactly what it feels like, but noticing it is a good first step.

It might take a few medications before you find the one that works. This is not an unusual process as everyone is different.

For chronic pain, you may find that there are few medications that completely get rid of the pain. It is more likely that it will get rid of some level of your everyday pain or dull it down, with you still experiencing 'breakthrough' pain.

There are several families of medications for most symptoms, and sometimes medicines normally used for another purpose are pre-scribed in specific doses for other issues, so you might find that you have to try a couple of different types for something that works for you.

It can also be the case that when you have several conditions, the medications that you need or that could be helpful may contraindicate. This is when medications or treatments should not be taken together or may impact you in negative ways, such as affecting your kidney function. This may mean your doctors have to consider which medication or treatment is more important for your health and quality of life.

You might find that medication isn't something you want to try at all, and that is okay too. Discuss this with your doctor. There are other ways to manage some symptoms, such as heat/cold, machines such as TENS and other aids. This will be discussed more in Chapters 2 and 3.

Experiencing side effects

Most doctors will ask you to try a medication for a few weeks before they take you off it or adjust the dosage, as side effects sometimes only last for a short while. However, if you are having very difficult side effects, you should get back into contact with them and make sure that these are not a bigger issue or something that you should be very worried about.

Whilst you should make sure you are informed about side effects of any new medications, try not to panic. Many of them are rare and only happen to a handful of people.

There are some side effects you may then be additionally medicated or treated for, such as being given anti-sickness meds for nausea.

Some of the side effects some medications cause can impact on your sensory issues if you have them. You may therefore find that you become more easily overwhelmed and need to take more time to look after your sensory needs, such as using sensory equipment or taking more breaks away from people.

Anxiety around taking medication

Medication might be a new thing to you, or you might have had negative experiences of it in the past. This is totally valid and not something that you should be ashamed of.

Make sure you ask your doctors any questions you have about the medication so that you have some of your worries eased before you begin to take them. There are also websites which can break down what medications are for and how they work, such as the guides produced by Young Minds about types of mental health medication.[6]

You might find it helpful to have someone with you for accountability when you take the medications (and they may also be able to support you to monitor any side effects). You might also like to have them with you when the doctor recommends the medications to ask any questions you might not have thought of, or to ease your worries.

As an autistic person you might also be more likely to struggle to take pills or swallow liquid due to your sensory needs. This is something you can talk to your doctor about and you can try different types. You might find it helpful to have medications which you could put into juice or yoghurt so that you don't have to handle the texture of the medications themselves.

If you are anxious about remembering to take your medication, there are lots of ways you can try and make sure that it is part of your routines. You could:

- set alarms
- put your meds next to something like your toothbrush to trigger the memory
- take them the moment you get up and place them next to your bed.

If you take multiple medications it can be particularly helpful to decant them into something like a dosette box each week so you do not miss any of the individual medications.

Navigating different elements of healthcare

Physiotherapy

Physiotherapy is something that many chronically ill people will be offered – sometimes a specialist for your condition, or maybe you will be sent to someone who is a more general physiotherapist to see if there is anything they can do to support your symptoms. Some people may see them as part of the diagnostic process to look at how your joints and muscles work.

As an autistic person, physiotherapy can be quite difficult for a few different reasons.

You might struggle with having someone touch you, or struggle with the coordination of the movements they ask you to do.

Jasper said:

> I've had physios who have been amazing and really considerate, where they have broken down steps or given me laminated sheets of my exercises. But I have also had physios that have been very hands on and made me feel like I know nothing about my condition.
>
> What made it better for me was that I started bringing someone with me to appointments to support me. I also made sure I had a five minute conversation on what I actually needed before we started, such as saying that I need you to break down the steps, demonstrate the exercise, and not touch me.

I also need information at the end of the appointment which is given directly so I know what to do after.

Don't try every type of management at once, if it's not working or causes a sensory issue you can try something else. For example, KT tape [a therapeutic kinesiology tape] causes me sensory issues so I have to be careful with it. – **Jasper**

Many also struggle to keep up with exercise regimes or stretches due to executive functioning differences or routine changes. It can be helpful to use reminders on your phone or to blue-tack reminders up around your house to do exercises as you go – I have a reminder for five heel raises next to my kitchen sink.

Some physiotherapists might be more aware of autism if they have come across patients with co-occurring conditions, but often they are not trained on neurodivergence.

MS is an autistic and ADHD person diagnosed with several mental illnesses that have a co-occurring physical impact, and a permanent meniscus tear in their ACL. They said:

When I had physiotherapy after getting ACL surgery, my low pain tolerance made it seem like I'm unreliable to describe my own pain as I was seen as exaggerating, and the healing process was done with less pain medication than I needed. It created more issues because I never completely healed from ACL though the surgery was done 13 years ago. – **MS**

The section in this chapter about interoception might help with discussing pain levels.

Psychological therapies[7]

A psychological therapy is not going to cure your chronic illness, but you may be offered it nonetheless. It might be helpful for some individuals, for reasons such as:

- Accepting your symptoms and diagnosis
- Understanding anxiety you may have surrounding being chronically ill
- Learning about who you are, or want to be
- Processing trauma, including medical trauma or medical gaslighting

You could be offered this separately to physical healthcare, or as a package with pain management support. There are different types of therapies and you may find some more useful than others.

Similarly, psychological therapies do not cure autism nor should this be implied or pushed by professionals; however, if you have associated anxiety, struggle with depression or have experienced trauma, you might find some psychological therapies helpful.

You might find some therapies harder to access or process as an autistic person, because they are generally built for allistic or neurotypical people. You might find that you struggle to focus on meditation, for example, or find that talking therapies don't have the structured approach that you might need.

It can help to find a therapist and/or type of therapy that works for you and is adapted for you. For example, art or music therapy may be more effective, or you might find that therapies like eye movement desensitisation and reprocessing (EMDR) or hypnotherapy work better. It will be different for everyone.

Some ways a therapist might be able to communicate with you in a way that is more effective for you might include:

- Using clear language and examples
- Taking the right pace
- Having structure within sessions or having an agenda
- Not using abstract concepts

You might also need more support to understand emotions due to alexithymia (struggling to describe your emotions) and therefore shouldn't be expected to always be able to put your emotions into specific wording.

The physical environment can also be important. If it is too bright in the room or there is noise outside, or the waiting room is busy, you might find it overwhelming or distressing, making it harder to access. Sometimes it might be small things that an allistic or neurotypical therapist might not consider, such as the ticking of a clock in the room, so it can help to discuss this with the therapist.

Examinations

Many autistic people may find being physically examined difficult for a variety of reasons, including:

- Sensory issues around touch and pain it can cause
- Not knowing what is going to happen
- Struggling to communicate about what is uncomfortable or difficult
- Being under- or over-stimulated by the examination

It might be useful beforehand to ask for clear guidance from the hospital or doctors about what will happen during the test to decrease levels of anxiety. For many examinations or types of testing, there may be accounts online about what happens from different charities or individuals who have previously experienced them.

Some of the ways that you can try and make these instances more comfortable could be:

- Wearing comfortable clothing
  - In some cases you might need to roll up your sleeves or the legs of your trousers, so you might find it helpful to wear something that easily rolls up.
- Asking the professional to tell you before they touch you, and tell you what they are going to do before it happens
- Having a conversation with the professional before they begin to touch you about your needs
  - You may want to inform them that you may need to take breaks or they may have to stop if it becomes difficult.
- Taking a stim toy or something comforting to manage your anxiety or making sure you can self-stimulate throughout
  - This might be a soft toy, something like a tangle, or taking your own pillow to lean on.

MRIs, scans and tests

There are a variety of tests and scans that you might have to experience as a chronically ill person, whether for diagnostic purposes, treatment or condition management.

MRI (magnetic resonance imaging) scans are where medical images are produced by a magnetic field and radio waves, to produce images of organs and tissue, often used to look at your brain or spine. You may have these as part of a diagnostic process, or if you are being treated to see if there has been progress.

MRIs are often very loud and may make you feel claustrophobic as you have to lie in the machine in what feels like a small tube. You might also have to be injected with a contrast dye depending on what they are looking for.

There are some ways that these can be made easier to cope with, such as:

- Wear clothes that contain no metal so you do not have to change when you get there – this includes making sure there is no metal in your bra, or a clasp on your trousers, for example. Some hospitals may prefer you to change into a gown, but they may allow you to not change as a reasonable adjustment.
- Normally there will be headphones which the radio is played into – sometimes you can change the station to make it more sensory friendly and right for you, and some may even let you bring your own music.
- You might be allowed to have a stim toy with you if it contains no metal, such as a tangle, but some may not allow this.
- If you have to have a contrast dye put in and might find this difficult, talk to the professional and make sure this process is taken more slowly.
- You generally cannot have someone come into the test room with you throughout, but as a reasonable adjustment someone should be able to come with you into the hospital to help you with any clothing changes and to settle your anxiety.
- You will be given a button to hold if the test gets too overwhelming – do not be afraid to use it if you need to.
- Make sure to take some time out after the test – you may feel overstimulated by the loud noises and might struggle to regulate yourself. It might be helpful to have a sensory break afterwards, so take items that comfort you with you to have in the car.

You may also have to have other scans, like a computerised tomography (CT or CAT) scan which uses a series of images to look inside the body. These ones are much quicker and not so noisy. You might still find it helpful to do some of the above things, like wearing sensory-friendly clothing and talking to the professional about what they can do to help.

Another test that can be quite difficult for autistic people is ultrasounds. These often use a wand which is pressed against your body, and a cool gel is often applied. This can be sticky and may cause sensory issues if you do not like sticky substances or gels touching you and your clothes. It can be quite difficult to deal with the wand being pressed onto you. Your technician should help you by making sure you aren't in pain and should help you take short breaks when possible. You might want to bring another set of clothes for afterwards so you feel cleaner, but they will give you some tissue to clean up the gel.

There are also several tests where you might have to prep for them or eat something as part of the test, such as a colonoscopy or gastric emptying studies. These can be difficult due to sensory needs as an autistic person. I asked autistic people to tell me how they have coped with these sorts of tests.

Some ways you might be able to make these more accessible might include:

- Ask for as much information as possible so you understand the whole process.
- Use your special interests to soothe you beforehand.
- Bring sensory regulation tools and distractions – some tests can take all day so it might help to download comfort shows or films.
- Talk to the staff and be upfront about any needs or anxieties.
- Make a schedule to work out when you need to do different aspects of the prep, and alarms to remind you.
- If you have to drink lots of water, it might be better to not travel with a full bladder. You could travel early and spend some time elsewhere whilst drinking the water, like a park.
- Prepare everything the day before and make sure you

have time to spare before you get there to ease any anxieties.

- If having to drink clear liquids, broth or stock may be preferred as it is salty and has flavour. If it can go in juice, don't pick your favourite or safe juice as you will go off it!
- If you have to eat a food (e.g. for gastric emptying), ask if you can choose it. You might be able to choose something that has a more preferable texture. Sometimes you can bring in safe foods for them to use.
- Talk to the team about sedation and painkillers. Sometimes autistic and/or chronically ill people don't experience sedation in the same way and we often experience pain differently.

Having surgery

Many chronically ill people may have to navigate surgeries, whether for reasons surrounding your chronic illnesses or for something acute. These can be difficult for autistic people due to anxiety surrounding surgery, changes to routines or changes to your lifestyle afterwards.

> I have had two surgeries for bowel prolapses and one to form my colostomy with another planned for 2023/2024. I think the main difficulties have been sensory with pain and discomfort, and the change of routine and not being able to do things I would usually do as part of my routine whilst recovering. This includes eating certain foods, exercising, working, etc... also the (greater) uncertainty of how I will feel every day means things become overwhelming very quickly. – **Adam**

Emily is a late-diagnosed autistic woman with ulcerative colitis and chronic back pain. She told me about how the logistics and anxiety of surgery were affected:

The last surgery I had was in June 2020, so during the pandemic. My anxiety was incredibly high about Covid safety during the procedure and I had to go into NYC for it. The anxiety around the travel, and how I would get safely there and back, was much more stressful than the procedure itself. Partly this was because I had to ask two different people for help in driving me, and I find it really difficult to ask for help.

This all happened before I was diagnosed as autistic, so it's one of those experiences (like many) that I am re-seeing through the lens of being autistic. At the time, I just felt generally panicked and couldn't think or speak very well, and I was in panic for days afterwards. Now I know that my routines and safety protocols were being super threatened, that I had to navigate complex social dynamics in a way that I wasn't comfortable doing, and I didn't know how to soothe myself at all. – **Emily**

Becky is autistic, disabled and chronically ill. She is an 18-year-old with Crohn's disease and POTS. She told me about how sensory issues impacted surgery:

I have had some minor surgeries due to my Crohn's disease. I have found preparations for these difficult due to the sensory issues caused by my autism... the preparation includes drinking multiple cups of diluted medicine, [and] the texture of these drinks is uncomfortable for me to swallow. This creates a very stressful 48 hours leading up to the surgery as I have to push myself through it. I also have struggled with these surgeries due to the uncertainty and worry around the surgeries due to unset timings causing me to become overwhelmed. As these surgeries were used for diagnosis and monitoring of my condition, I often experienced a lot of worry causing me to become upset. – **Becky**

Navigating Accident and Emergency departments and Emergency Rooms

If you need to access Accident and Emergency (A&E, or Emergency Room) services for any reason, this can be an overwhelming experience as it is often busy, with long wait times, people bustling around and lots of machines beeping. There are some objects you might find it useful to have when going to A&E. If you have to attend regularly, you might want to consider making a prepared bag for this situation. Sometimes you may not know you are going to attend, but if you are going from home, you could take:

- Ear defenders, headphones or earplugs to block out the noises
- Stim and fidget toys to regulate with
- Pyjamas and a change of clothes in case you stay overnight
- Objects that comfort you, like soft toys
- A phone charger
- A toothbrush and paste, and deodorant, so you don't have to deal with the sensory feelings of feeling unclean
- Anything that you need to make sure you are comfortable and can regulate your sensory needs – for example, a water bottle with a straw, or a hairbrush and bobbles if your hair gets overwhelming

Autism and disability awareness in A&E

Many of us have experiences in A&E where staff struggle to understand autistic patients, and they may also misunderstand those attending for their chronic illness symptoms. This can be frustrating and if you are already in crisis or need medical help, this may be distressing.

Harriet is a 22-year-old who is autistic, dyspraxic and has PCOS. She has been to A&E several times due to ovarian cyst ruptures and said:

> As an autistic person, I struggle with interoception and this has often made it difficult to correctly identify and communicate key areas of pain, or to successfully 'describe' pain when prompted by nurses. Working with pain scales is also tricky for me, and each time I have visited A&E I have been asked to rate the severity my pain out of 10. Due to my low sensitivity to pain and my confusion at the use of the scale and what each number might mean, I consistently under-report my pain levels. I would not even know I was doing this if it weren't for my mom, who has attended A&E with me each time and had to correct me to the doctors; she does this because she is aware of my confusion and, after witnessing me throw up for hours from the pain, knows that the issue is more serious than I might be conveying.
>
> This presents a problem, though, because doctors and nurses seem to be suspicious of her correcting me and start to question my illness. A lack of understanding of autistic communication differences and difficulties means that they are not accepting of my mom as someone who will help me to effectively communicate my pain, especially now that I am an adult. – **Harriet**

Elli is disabled and chronically ill, and has Type 1 diabetes, hypermobility and other associated conditions. She talked about navigating A&E around her blood glucose levels:

I forget my medications or diagnoses, and so have a cue card now to give new HCAs [healthcare assistants]. I've found it works really well with paramedics and in A&E because all the info is in one place and then they can just plug it into their computers. I also get very pedantic when my blood glucose is low, and I have been considered to be rude and belligerent (masking stops when my blood glucose is low!) so HCAs ignore me until something is really wrong. I make sure to take all my own hypo treatments with me so I can treat myself because I don't trust HCAs to know enough about diabetes. – **Elli**

We will discuss interoception and pain in more detail in Chapter 3. Masking refers to when autistic people 'camouflage' their autistic traits to fit in better – it is often unconscious and something many of us don't realise we are doing. In an emergency situation, you might find you do this less, like Elli, because your brain and body are navigating so many different things, or you might find you do it more because your brain is using it as a survival mechanism. We will discuss masking in more depth in Chapter 8.

Whilst it should be the responsibility of healthcare professionals to learn about autism, you might find that you feel less anxious if you prepare for a possible lack of understanding in advance, especially if you have to attend A&E often.

Some ideas you could think about implementing to make this process smoother include:

- Having communication cards that you can show for different situations, such as having a meltdown, not being able to speak or being overwhelmed

- Having a printed one-page profile or detailed medical ID on your phone that tells them about your support needs and conditions
- Wearing a sunflower lanyard or other indicator which alerts people that you have a hidden disability. You could add badges or a card on the end of it to add more detail, or wear a bracelet that allows for a few lines about what you need
- If you, like me, struggle to describe pain or use numerical scales, work out how comfortable you are to tell them about this and see if you can think of an alternative

Chey is a chronically ill and autistic person with PCOS and HS. They are also a nurse, and said:

> Most professionals are very good at their allocated 'thing' [speciality] and then know a little about everything else in order to provisionally test and refer. I have seen poor understanding of a condition, such as autism, lead to fractious communication and poor outcomes for both staff and patient.
>
> My advice: have a 'This Is Me' document, or similar, prepared to take with you.[8] The document is free to download and was designed for patients with neurological disorders such as dementia, so if you can, adapt it or make your own version! Pick questions it uses that work for you; add questions that would help you if you were unable to verbally communicate your needs – because that is what *so much* of healthcare relies on. – **Chey**

KEY TAKEAWAYS FROM THIS CHAPTER

- Communicating differently is not shameful and should be validated and supported in healthcare settings.
- There are lots of different things that might help you to access medical care, such as advocates or alternative forms of communication.
- Many autistic people have differences with interoception, meaning you process pain or body sensations differently – this doesn't mean you aren't experiencing them or don't deserve support with them.
- Diagnosis or discovery of a condition can lead to many mixed emotions, and it may take time to figure them out.
- Finding the right medications, treatments or supports is different for everyone.

Example one-page profile

❗ IMPORTANT INFORMATION:

Full name:. . . . .

Date of birth: . . . .

Address:. . . . .

Emergency contact: . . . .

Conditions/diagnoses:	When to call an ambulance:
Medications & treatments:	Access or communication needs:
Allergies & reactions:	My interests & hobbies:

2

Everyday life

Although other chapters of this book will focus on specific elements of being autistic and chronically ill that definitely impact life every day, it felt key to have a chapter about some of the aspects of life that are seen as 'everyday', that can be more difficult and impacted by our conditions, like chores and errands.

Every chronically ill and autistic person will be impacted around these sorts of things differently, so it isn't as simple as providing some top tips which fit everyone. This chapter will detail some of the ways you might be able to adapt things or put additional help in place. Some autistic chronically ill individuals may not be able to do these things at all and will need more help to do them – that's also totally valid. A lot of these tasks are made difficult by not just the traits we experience as a result of being disabled, but the barriers society puts in place too.

I have written most of this chapter with the theoretical situation in mind that you can't afford someone to help you or your family and friends can't do so. For many of us, we might have some form of support that doesn't require our energy, whether that be from a personal relationship or from social care or a personal assistant, but I wanted to provide some ideas in the case that you don't have this, or in case you are wanting more ideas for independence – or if you are the adult of the family, for example! It is therefore worth bearing in mind that there may be other ways that you handle everyday living, and those are totally valid too, if they work for you.

The overarching idea of this chapter is: find what works for you and know that it is valid! You know yourself best and you shouldn't be ashamed of finding ways for an inaccessible society to work for you.

Memory

I want to open this chapter with talking about memory and executive functioning differences because it is something that affects all the different parts of everyday life we will go on to talk about.

Memory can be impacted in multiple ways as an autistic and chronically ill person, whether that be due to executive function differences, brain fog or memory loss, for example. Many of us also have co-occurring ADHD or dyspraxia, which can also impact memory.

It may impact your short-term memory, long-term memory, recall, or it may vary. Sometimes it may be situational, for example if you are in sensory overwhelm or during a flare-up. You could find it hard to form sentences or lose your train of thought.

This isn't something to be ashamed of. Society often makes us feel embarrassed for difficulties with memory, but they are more common than you might think.

Some ways you might be able to support difficulties with memory include:

- Using visual aids, like sticking up reminders around the house, or having timetables to support
- Having specific places to put certain things, such as a hook for your keys by the door

- Using aids like apps or tags that track location of items you commonly lose
- Writing down anything you commonly forget, like appointments, or using apps to track symptoms or questions you have for doctors

Cooking

Cooking can be a particularly huge minefield for many autistic and chronically ill people for a variety of reasons, from the fine motor skills needed, to the exhaustion you might experience from prepping, to the executive function of knowing what to cook. Some things that might be helpful for lessening the issues this causes might be:

- Cooking additional portions of meals and putting them in the fridge or freezer so you don't have to cook as often or have lunch prepared for the next day (you can do this easily by doubling quantities of all ingredients).
- Buying ready meals, frozen foods and pre-prepared foods for when you have less capacity, as well as buying pre-cut or portioned ingredients such as frozen peppers and onions, or tinned potatoes. You can even buy jars of ingredients like garlic or chilli so you don't have to prepare them.
- Having a stool in the kitchen to sit on, or sitting down at the table whilst chopping things up or between steps.
- Having equipment that supports your needs, such as utensils with thicker handles, swing colanders, kettle tippers, electric tin openers, or angled measuring jugs.
- Using multiple timers for each item that is cooking – if your phone doesn't provide this capability, there are apps that allow for this or you could use physical timers.
- Having a plan for what meals you will have, or having recipes easily available for when you are struggling to

think of what you want. If they have pictures, this might help you to visualise the task and more easily process when struggling with your executive function.

- Using a food box service where ingredients come pre-portioned for pre-determined recipes, so you have fewer steps to navigate.
- Cooking meals that are made in one pan or pot, so there is less cleaning and fewer aspects to try and manage, or avoiding meals that require lots of attention all throughout the process to make sure you can rest between steps (like risottos for example).

I find it very difficult to know what I want to eat, and this makes every part of the process difficult, from the food shop to the cooking itself. I have quite a limited diet so have found it helpful to have meals that I know I can fall back on that I want to eat and are easy to cook, but it might also help to have some cookbooks or follow some food bloggers, Instagrammers or TikTokers, for example, to get more ideas if you are feeling adventurous or stuck.

For many autistic and chronically ill people, a microwave can be your best friend, as there are lots of things you can easily make in shorter times and with fewer steps to do so. Similarly, many may find an air fryer more easily accessible for them than a normal convection oven, as they are not heavy and can make small amounts of food much more quickly and without as much cleaning as an oven tray would need. Lastly, a slow cooker might also be a good tool, as you don't have to do as much maintenance of the meal once it is prepped – and you can prep it earlier or at a point in the day where you have more energy, rather than trying to make it in the evening when you might be struggling more after navigating the rest of the day.

If you are able to do so, it can help to have the kitchen structured in ways that help you – for example, having hooks on the wall or knifes on a magnet strip so that you can see them and grab them more easily. This is not simple for everyone due to factors like renting, for example, but it may be helpful to consider what you can do to make the kitchen make more sense and feel less overwhelming and cluttered. Storing things in categories that make sense to you can also help, or making sure heavy or fragile items are more accessible and not high up.

It can be helpful to prep for the entirety of the task before you start – having all your equipment ready and grouped together for easy access and prepping ingredients so you don't have to look for equipment as you go or have to continually start new processes. This can help your executive functioning differences and might mean you use the most energy at the start, so the rest of the process is easier when you are running out of energy.

It can also help to make sure your body is not taking the strain from any tools you are using. If your knives or scissors are blunt you might have to use more energy to use them, or it might exacerbate pain you already have. It can also help to have tools like an electric whisk or blender, for example, so that there is less for you to physically have to manage.

I have talked online before about how ultimately eating is better than not eating – even if you are eating the same food repeatedly or your meal is made up of multiple snacks, that's better than eating nothing at all. Whilst it might not be ideal long term or every single day, in that moment, as a disabled person, something is better than nothing, and it isn't something that you should be ashamed of.

I have a lot of one-pot meals in my head, and I have all the recipes I might need in a clip on my fridge. I saved up for 'gadgets' that make my food situation easier, so for example I have an air fryer so that I can do frozen vegetables or

frozen meat really easily. This means I don't have to gro-
cery shop as often, AND frozen vegetables are much more
predictable in terms of their texture. Also since the air fryer
is waist height, I don't have to bend over to get things out
of the oven.

I have microwave frozen meals that I know I love, for when I
can't do anything else. Moving near a Trader Joe's has made
my life a lot better in some really concrete ways.

I keep a pretty regular schedule for eating (10am English
muffin! 3pm protein bar!) and that helps a lot too, especially
with the colitis. – **Emily**

Eating and drinking itself will be discussed more in Chapter 3, where
we discuss sensory needs. There are a host of reasons eating and
drinking can be hard, including our interoception issues (not knowing whether we are hungry or not) and sensory aversions.

For more discussion about cooking as an autistic person, you might
want to read *The Autistic Friendly Cookbook* by Lydia Wilkins (2022).

Getting dressed

Getting dressed – one of the tasks you generally have to do in the
morning – can be difficult particularly when you are struggling to
transition into the daytime. It can also be physically difficult, as
adaptive clothing is still often rarely available or financially accessible, and many clothes can be difficult to put on, cause pain or
cause sensory issues.

Autistic people are often tactile defensive or struggle with hypersensitivity to touch,[1] which can make dressing much more difficult.

It can make us not want to have something touching our skin, including clothes – and this can then be compounded by our chronic pain or difficulties with skin feeling itchy or hot as a result of also being chronically ill. For example, many of us might struggle with the seams in our socks or the labels in our clothes, which are much less likely to overly bother our non-disabled peers.

One of the most obvious ways to support yourself with getting dressed is trying to have clothing that meets some of your more pressing needs. For me, sensory-friendly clothing is a priority, as well as that without tough buttons which I struggle with due to the pain in my fingers combined with my fine motor issues. For you, it might be that you can't do laces or tie knots, struggle with belts, or you have a stoma bag or catheter. Finding clothes which prioritise your needs rather than the comfort of others can be an important step in supporting yourself.

However, sometimes it isn't that simple. Sometimes we might have to be wearing a specific type of clothing for an event, or it might be harder to find size-inclusive clothes that meet your needs, or they simply don't exist.

A few ways you might be able to support yourself with getting dressed might include:

- Set out your clothes the night before or have a plan for which clothes you will wear to avoid getting overwhelmed in the mornings. Some people use apps or physical photos to plan this and have it in front of them.
  - A capsule wardrobe can be helpful for some autistic people, so they don't have so many clothes that they don't know where to start.
- Use aids such as zip pulls or shoe horns.
- Find clothing which isn't officially adaptive but meets your needs. For example, front clasp bras, all-in-one clothing, or clothes with easy buckles. You might need

looser fitting clothing if you have medical equipment underneath, or you might prefer tighter fitting clothes for sensory reasons.

- Work out what sorts of things you struggle with when getting dressed. You might find pulling things over your head is easier than the buttons of shirts, or vice versa, for example.
- Remember that needing adaptations does not make you childish – for example, using Velcro rather than laces or zips.

Some autistic and chronically ill people may find it helpful to have multiples of the same clothing, whether that be exactly the same or in different colours or patterns. This can be helpful to make getting dressed more comfortable and feel safer, knowing the clothes meet your needs and speed up the process of transitioning in the mornings or going elsewhere, such as to work. For example, my wardrobe is primarily made up of the same dungarees in different colours, T-shirts and soft hoodies. It means I use less brain space on knowing what to wear and means I can spend that energy elsewhere.

In some cases there are more unconventional ways of supporting these needs. For instance, I know several wheelchair users who wear maternity jeans because normal jeans dig into their stomachs whilst they are sat down.

Getting undressed at the end of the day can also be difficult for similar reasons regarding transitioning to a new set of clothes, and sometimes our symptoms can be worse after a day of activity, making us more resistant to doing so or simply unable to do so. It might be helpful to put your pyjamas or night clothes alongside other aspects of your night routine, such as medications or skincare, and to make sure that these are easy to put on. Some may find it hard to put away their day clothes, so it can be worth finding a system that works for you when it comes to this – for example, I don't tend to put pressure on myself to put them away until the next day; others have a box or bag to dump them in.

Laundry

Of course, getting dressed also means producing laundry which has to be done eventually. For me, this is one of the harder tasks – there are so many steps to it and there's always just so much of it to be done!

Some of the ways to ease this task could include:

- Have multiple small laundry baskets, rather than one big one, to transport laundry, or find one which has wheels.
- Alternatively, you could put your laundry basket directly next to the washing machine (or you could even put your washing directly into the machine as you need to, if no-one uses it between washes!).
- Use pods or gels which go into the machine, rather than having to lift heavy bottles or boxes to put in the drawer.
- Use colour catchers and put all your laundry into one load instead of separating it, or if you want to separate it, have two separate laundry baskets so this task is done before you go to actually wash it.
- Use a scent which you like, or scentless products, to make sure you don't have a sensory aversion to the task or to your clothes.
- Use net laundry bags (sometimes known as micro-filter bags) or delicates bags to keep different types of clothes separate within the machine to lessen the task of grouping everything afterwards.
- Use a tool such as a grabber to make sure you can reach clothing at the back of the machine that has gotten stuck in the process.
- Have multiple sets of bigger items like towels or bedding,

so there is less pressure to get this washed and dried immediately when it needs changing around.

Many chronically ill and autistic people are prone to more skin sensitivities, or may have mast cell activation syndrome or histamine allergies, meaning it can be harder to find products which don't trigger you. Chemical-free or fragrance-free products may help this – it may sometimes be easier to find chemical-free ones by looking for those marketed as eco-friendly, though this is not a fail-safe way of doing so.

Once the laundry is done, it can be difficult to then transfer this to a tumble dryer or to a drying rack. Some people have machines which do both of these functions to prevent having to move clothes when they are heavier due to being wet, but many won't be able to access one of these. If these machines can be directly next to each other, this can make the process easier – but make sure the hinges are on the correct sides to not place a door barrier between the two. It could also help to have a basket on wheels to transfer between the two, rather than having to make multiple trips.

Once dry, the process of transferring clothes back to its storage can also be a monumental task, particularly if you struggle with executive dysfunction as an autistic person. Some of the tips I've heard for this include:

- Having open storage so you don't have to navigate opening doors, such as using drawers or baskets
- Having hangers that are designed for saving space, as you can put away multiple clothes at once rather than reaching multiple times
- Doing this task whilst watching TV or listening to a podcast, to give yourself some other sensory input
- Having all matching socks so you don't have to pair them up (i.e. all white socks or all black socks)

- Making yourself feel less pressure to iron or fold clothing
- Remembering that it doesn't have to be put away immediately! Sometimes you might be too tired from the other stages and that's okay (however, other individuals may find it more helpful to get it all done immediately to complete the task)

Taking care of personal hygiene

Personal hygiene is another area that autistic and chronically ill people can struggle with for reasons that are from both of their needs combined. From sensory aversion to joint pain and dizziness, as well as executive functioning differences, there are a lot of possibilities for why you might find this area more difficult. This area can include everything from brushing your teeth, to showering or bathing, to managing periods or cutting your nails.

Although everyone is different, some tips that might help you to consider your needs and begin to support them include:

- Find out which toiletries are sensory friendly for you by getting samples or buying travel-size bottles.
- Buy toiletries which help you to sensory seek and/or don't lead to sensory aversion, for example scents you enjoy.
- Use shampoo caps, dry shampoo or baby wipes if you can't take a full shower or wash your hair.
- Use a shower chair if you struggle to stand up during showers or find that you feel dizzy afterwards. It can help to have had some water and salt before you shower to help prevent this too.
- Buy toiletry bottles which have hand pumps, or replace lids with them, so you don't have to squeeze bottles.
- Consider which tools make personal hygiene accessible to you. For example, a sponge may be preferable for

sensory reasons, or something with a long handle may be helpful for joint support.

- Schedule in personal hygiene tasks or use visual supports to help you with any overwhelm you are feeling about the task. You might find it helpful to timeblock rest after these tasks if you struggle with energy levels or symptoms affected by them.
- Listen to music or a podcast whilst doing hygiene tasks to distract you if you find it unpleasant or overwhelming.
- Try to change clothing or pyjamas regularly even if you are at home or in bed. This can make you feel fresher.
- Try unscented or unflavoured products.

We will specifically discuss periods in Chapter 3 during the discussion of sensory needs, including tips on how to manage these.

There are lots of different adaptive tools for personal hygiene for disabled people out there. You might find that if you work with an occupational therapist that you try these out or are given them. Otherwise, if you can afford to, they are available to buy online or from mobility shops, and these might be helpful for you to consider using.

I know some chronically ill and autistic people who partially manage their personal hygiene through services, for example going to a spa, or getting a manicure and pedicure if they struggle with managing their nails. Obviously, this is not something everyone can afford or access – but it is another novel way of managing your needs that can work for some, as it relieves pressure and is more normalised in our current, often ableist society.

It is worth remembering that a lot of norms that society preaches about personal hygiene are often not as crucial or accurate as they are made out to be – for example, showering every day is not necessary in the way many describe or sneer about, particularly when you have conditions which make you struggle with this. Using other ways of keeping clean are perfectly valid. It is not as simple as *wanting* to engage with personal hygiene tasks – for us, there is way more than this at play and there is absolutely no shame in this.

Going to the toilet

For our non-disabled peers, it's unlikely that they would even have to think twice about going to the toilet – for many of us, it's more complex than that. As an autistic person, our hyposensitivity to interoception can mean we don't think about it often or until it is too late, and as chronically ill people many of us experience a variety of difficulties with our bladders or bowels, from incontinence to constipation to having urinary tract infections more often, or struggling to undress to go to the toilet.

None of these symptoms or factors are anything to be ashamed of – but society would still like you to think that they are. We will discuss this a bit more in Chapter 7 when we talk about ableism and internalised ableism, but it is worth saying here that you are not 'gross' for having issues with this.

The needs here will be different for everyone experiencing them. Some might have a catheter or a stoma, both of which are discussed in Chapter 3. Others may have needs more surrounding the interoception aspect. It can help to have routines around going to the toilet rather than relying on body signals, like going at specific times of day or using 'habit stacking', where you go to the bathroom before or after another task to trigger your memory.

Cleaning

I don't know many people who really like cleaning, but we are likely to face additional barriers with this, whether practical, sensory or motivational. I am definitely not the best at cleaning, and it is often a bit neglected in my life, which is why many of the tips I'm providing in this particular section are crowdsourced.

Some of the ways I support myself with cleaning tasks are:

- Using a mini handheld vacuum rather than trying to navigate a normal vacuum cleaner (there are also robot ones out there which can also use limited energy)
- Using antibacterial wipes and sprays
- Using a sponge with a handle for washing up, as I don't like being submerged in water
- Trying to clean up little and often rather than having to do bigger cleans because they're more tiring and overwhelming (this is not foolproof...)
- Soaking dishes first so I have to use less energy scrubbing (but they do need washing eventually, unfortunately)
- Sitting down to do tasks like sorting or doing dishes

Some other tips for cleaning include:

- Using a duster and mops with an extended handle so you can sit down/not have to stretch
- Having a cleaning rota to encourage you to do one task a day instead of lots at once
- Using a dishwasher if you have one to reduce energy – and unload it later or the next day
- Having trays/boxes to drop things into in each room that need taking into another room, or using tools like bedside hanging storage to keep specific needed items in one place

- Using gloves if you struggle with touch aversion or if you are sensitive to chemicals
- Having a grabber tool to pick stuff up without bending or to get things out of reach
- Having visual reminders of what tasks need to be done, and having step-by-step methods for those which take multiple steps

In Chapter 4, which is all about pacing, we will discuss more about spacing out tasks and not exhausting yourself through doing too much, which can often be applied to cleaning.

Some autistic and chronically ill people have mentioned that they find minimalism helpful to making their life easier when it comes to cleaning, organisation and overwhelm. Whilst not a lifestyle that works for everyone when it comes to every part of their life, it could be applied to smaller areas, such as having less kitchen equipment, having fewer toiletries, or having a capsule wardrobe, for example.

If your issues with cleaning surround motivation or executive function, you might find it helpful to gamify your cleaning or add another sensory stimuli to it – for example, seeing how much you can do in 20 minutes, using a timer, watching a decluttering/productivity video alongside it, or seeing how much you can do during an episode of a podcast. A common technique that is often used with ADHD folk but can also help autistic people is body doubling – when you are alongside another person to encourage you to stay focused and make you more aware of what you are doing.

Just like with personal hygiene, sometimes cleaning tasks simply aren't going to be the top priority you have if you're just trying to survive, and you need to give yourself the space to know that this is okay! I know lots of chronically ill and autistic folks who manage some of their needs through sometimes using things like paper plates when they cannot keep up – this isn't a personal or moral failure.

Running errands

There are lots of errands that can come with being an autistic and chronically ill human, particularly when you get to adult life – including both those which are specific to your disabilities and those which come more generally with living life. Lots of these can be difficult due to our anxiety, autistic inertia, executive functioning differences or how much energy they can take up.

With technology and society the way it is now, there are a lot more errands that can be done online in your own home – you can buy most things online to have delivered, including your food shopping, which might be helpful to you as a chronically ill and autistic person.

I personally find clothes shopping very difficult in person, but I then often have to make returns due to them not meeting my sensory needs or just being the wrong size or shape. I tend to try and find the most accessible way the shop will allow me to do this, whether that is going to the post office or returning via another means available like postal lockers. Some services may collect from your home, which might also be better for you. If you are like me and likely to forget to do this before the return window ends, setting multiple reminders or putting the parcel by your door can be helpful.

This is the same for going to the post office in general. There are delivery services that may pick up mail from you, but you may have to go yourself. In these instances, I find it helpful to make sure I know all the information they will ask me – what class or type it will be going (first class, signed for) and where. Some will ask for an idea of what is inside, to make sure it is not violating any rules, but you can find lists of restricted items online too.

Another common errand that I struggle with is going to the bank. Many banks now have apps where you can do the majority of your banking, or there are banks that are totally online, such as fintech banks, which might be more accessible to you. If you do have to physically go to the bank, for example if your bank makes you pay in cheques or cash that way, some autistic people might find it helpful to ask a worker for support, whilst others may prefer to use machines independently.

Money management and budgeting

Many chronically ill and autistic people face difficulties with money, including budgeting and managing it.

Some of the issues that can come up for us around money include (but are not limited to):

- Lack of income or variable income if you can't work or can only work sometimes
- Having lots of additional costs for your disabilities, varying from condition management or medications to things like takeaways for when you are struggling or having to buy branded food due to sensory needs
- Lack of energy or executive function meaning managing money slips your mind or isn't a priority
- Difficulties with memory making you struggle to remember where your cards are, what you've spent or when payments are due
- Access to benefits (or lack of) or other financial support for disabled people

We will discuss difficulties of working itself more in Chapter 5, which partially focuses on employment, including reasonable adjustments and working from home.

There is no single answer to money management and budgeting, especially when dealing with the overlapping and clashing issues being autistic and chronically ill can provide in this situation. A lot of budgeting advice is very focused on a standard, regular income, and relies on a lack of executive functioning differences or the ability to go to lots of different shops to find different prices, which isn't accessible to many of us.

I am yet to find a proper system that works for me, however a couple of the things that help me are:

- Writing down in multiple places when my bills go out or are due and when subscriptions will be taken
- Using functions my bank offers, such as rounding up payments and saving the remaining amount (e.g. if I spend 83p, 17p will go to my savings)
- Using apps that manage savings for me, taking regular savings from my bank account (I use Plum)
  - There are several 'savings challenges' that some people do to help them save without having to think about it, such as the £1 challenge or 1p challenge
- Making sure I regularly look at my bank account so I can visualise the amount of money I have better
- Buying my safe foods in bulk so even if I have to buy branded products they are slightly cheaper
- Bookmarking items I want to buy and leaving them there for a few days to check that I actually want them
- Checking that I am getting any benefits I'm entitled to or any grants or bursaries from my place of education

When I am in a better place financially I also sometimes put a percentage of any income straight into my savings, however this is not always possible.

In some situations, a subscription is preferable as you don't have to think about it and sometimes when it is a product it means you don't have to use energy going out to get something – for example I have a subscription for my razors. However, in other situations, one-off payments may be better as you might forget to cancel a subscription or may only need those items periodically.

Some autistic and chronically ill people may find it better not to have an overdraft or credit card so they are less likely to fall into debt, but others may need this in order to pay for disability-related costs, so consider what's right for you.

Some crowdsourced ideas around budgeting and money management include:

- Creating and adding to an emergency fund for any unexpected costs, whether they be health related or general life
- Opening available financial support systems, such as ISAs
- Using cashback websites
- Buying frozen and canned food during food shops just after payday so there is food left if you are struggling at the end of the month
- Putting all of your income into your savings and putting small amounts into your main account each week or as needed, so you are less able to splurge and can visualise your budget more easily

Going to the dentist

Going to the dentist is not necessarily an 'everyday' activity, but it is a part of life we have to handle. For many, it will be twice a year check-ups, but many autistic and chronically ill people are more likely to have issues with their teeth and mouth health. This could be because of struggling with teeth brushing for sensory or physical reasons, or related to your chronic illness itself.

We discussed teeth brushing in the personal hygiene section, but going to the dentist can be a mammoth task as it is a very difficult sensory situation, can lead to increased anxiety and can be painful. A lot of people often avoid going to the dentist because of these reasons, which can cause worse problems down the line.

It is nothing to be ashamed of if this is very difficult for you. Many dentists are not aware of disabled patients' needs and can often not help with this situation.

However, there may be ways that the dentist can support you to manage appointments, many of which are only small adjustments. These could include:

- Allowing you to wear ear defenders, earplugs or noise cancelling headphones to reduce the impact of noise from equipment
- Allowing you to use a sensory toy such as a tangle or stress ball
- Letting someone come into the room with you and be near you if this is preferred
- Extending your appointments to allow for a slower appointment pace to reduce anxiety and allow time for explaining processes to you
  - This might also mean putting treatments into another appointment rather than springing them on you during the check-up
- Using flavourless products and mouthwashes
- Having visuals of treatments or of things they are trying to explain to you
- Making sure light is as far away as possible or blocked out where it can be; this is difficult as they need it to work, but some may have thoughts on how they can adjust it or let you wear your own sunglasses instead of their glasses to try and help this

Some dentists can find ways to look into your mouth without

touching it as much. Not every dentist will be confident or trained to do so. If this is something you find very difficult, you could talk to your dentist about being referred to someone who can. There are also some dentists out there who specifically work with disabled or anxious patients.

It can also help some autistic people to not have to wait in the main waiting room, which is applicable to other types of appointments too. They might be able to put you in a quieter room or allow you to wait outside until the time of your appointment.

If your dentist doesn't seem to understand autism or your chronic illnesses, it might help you to have an explanation handy if you are anxious, have someone with you to explain them, or you could even print something off which helps explain it to them. Some dentists will have had training on this, but it is not always effective and others might not have had any at all.

Getting a haircut

Hairdressers or barbers and haircuts can be particularly difficult for a variety of reasons, including dealing with the sensory aspects both of the environment and being touched, having to make small talk, and having to deal with pain from sitting up or from leaning back to have your hair washed.

Some autistic and chronically ill people might find it easier to cut their own hair or have a family member cut it (or not cut it at all!). Sometimes your area might have a hairdresser who can come to your house to make it more comfortable.

If this isn't possible, you might be able to find ways to make going to a hairdresser or barber easier. For example, it may be preferable to have a dry cut if you struggle with having your hair washed.

You can also take sensory regulation tools and you could try going at off-peak times.

Some autistic and chronically ill people prefer to keep their hair short so they have to do less to manage it on a day-to-day basis.

Hobbies and sports

Hobbies, interests and activities can be really difficult to manage as an autistic and chronically ill individual. Sometimes something might be autistic friendly, but will exacerbate symptoms of the illness; contrastingly, something might be accessible for you physically but too difficult for you for sensory reasons, for example.

It's important to remember that you are allowed to have joy in this life as a chronically ill and autistic person. We talk more about pacing in Chapter 4, but it is worth noting here that it's important to allow yourself time and capacity for joy – and you shouldn't feel guilty if that takes more of your energy, leaving less for other tasks.

Most autistic people have special interests. Even though the term includes 'interests', these are not always specific topics, but sometimes activities and sports too. Regardless of what they are, engaging with them is not always easy as a chronically ill person for similar reasons as to engaging with any other hobby or interest. The following tips should also apply to some special interests, but we'll discuss them more specifically in Chapter 4.

Although not every chronically ill autistic person will be able to engage in lots of hobbies, sports or activities outside the home in traditional ways like attending clubs, many might have at-home hobbies, be able to access them elsewhere, or can find ways to adapt traditional environments. Either way, there are definitely some ways to try out, adapt and engage with hobbies, such as:

- Finding online groups or discussing your hobbies on your own platforms on social media
- Going along to sessions with a friend or someone trusted so you don't feel alone or worried that something will happen without support
- Trying out activities you can do at home, such as crafting – some people have found subscription services or borrowing from someone else helpful for this to try out a variety of ideas until they can find what they like
- Finding activities that you can do from bed to conserve energy, such as origami, language learning, online courses, puzzles or watching documentaries
- Trying accessible sports, like wheelchair basketball

Many of us may find that our hobbies we used to have become less accessible if our conditions worsen – although many hobbies or sports can be adapted for you to continue to engage somehow, this is not always the case for everything. This is not an easy situation to be in and can make you angry, bitter or upset – I have certainly been all of those things. I won't pretend that this isn't hard. You will often need time to process and grieve this before you can try to find something to replace it.

Sleeping

Insomnia is very common in autistic individuals, and sleep can also be disturbed as a chronically ill individual by your symptoms or treatments. I experience painsomnia often, where pain is heightened at night and keeps me up, and my fatigue sometimes takes the form of being so exhausted that I can no longer sleep. Many also experience sleep disturbances throughout the night, rather than not being able to get to sleep to start with, or they may have to run certain treatments during the night that may keep them up.

My chronic illness includes muscle and joints disorders (and permanent leg injury). It is very hard for me to fall asleep not only because of my brain activities and the co-existing sleep abnormality in autism, but it could be a physically painful experience. I would often wake up with joint pain or muscle cramps, and sometimes it disabled me to physically get up for the first hour after waking up. I have to make sure that the surface is safe for me to lie down for a long time, right texture of beddings (from sensory needs), and I always need auditory inducement (like brown noise or ASMR), and sometimes even sleeping pills to be able to fall asleep. – **MS**

I find that bad sleep significantly feeds my chronic pain and fatigue as well as my anxiety and sensory overwhelm. My sleep is the foundation of everything for me, and this is often the case for autistic and chronically ill people. We can end up in a cycle of bad sleep causing symptoms and these symptoms then causing the bad sleep to continue. It is not a simple problem to solve, and it can be difficult to make mental health professionals understand and take into account the physical health impact and vice versa.

For some, there may not be many ways to support your sleep yourself beyond a certain point, and instead medication may be necessary whether that be melatonin to support production of the hormone, or a sleeping pill. This should be worked on with your doctor. Similarly, those with chronic pain may need pain medication in the evening to help night-time pain.

There are other ways you can help yourself with your sleep or making the night more comfortable if you can't physically sleep. Traditional 'sleep hygiene' often promoted by the medical sector might not work for you as a disabled individual. Our differences in processing sensory input and generally being wired differently can mean those ideas don't gel with you or don't help. Warm milk and baths might help some people, but don't be too worried if these aren't enough for you.

However, here are some things that might help you with sleeping or night-time:

- Use of white or brown noise or earplugs to manage auditory needs
- Blocking out light with blackout curtains
- Having blankets, covers and pyjamas that are sensory friendly (this might include taking off labels, using detergent you like, and bedding being consistent)
- Journaling or planning the next day before bed so you don't have so many thoughts running through your head
- Trying different pillows and supports, such as batwing or V pillows for your back, or a 'pregnancy' full body pillow to support your joints; some might need a specific type of mattress to support the body effectively, or you might find it helpful to not sleep totally flat
- Having activities you can do if you can't sleep that won't stimulate the brain too much, like reading (possibly with an e-reader if you struggle to hold books), colouring in or puzzles
- Using sunset lights to encourage your brain to understand the transition into night-time
- Trying to sleep at the same time each night; you might not get to sleep, but it encourages the body to understand the time of day

Bedtime is a place where sensory needs and chronic illness really intersect. I need to get a certain amount of sleep for my physical health, and I need really specific temperature/texture/weight as I sleep. So I've got my favourite pillow, humidifier, etc. etc. I also need to be able to take

a lot of time in the bathroom in the evenings and I've set up my bathroom with nice lighting, a pretty set of prints, etc. so that I feel soothed while I'm there. Harsh bathroom lights right before bed would mean a terrible night's sleep.
– **Emily**

It can be helpful if you are not asleep after a period of time to get up and move around a little bit to try and reset the bedtime. I often find myself too wired and awake for hours at a time. It might help to go to the toilet, distract yourself for a while or stretch. When you feel sleepy again, then you can try to go back to bed again.

Research has shown that autistic people can be more likely to experience delayed sleep phases, where our optimal bedtime is hours later than 'conventional' bedtimes.[2] You might find that it is better for your sleep patterns to go to bed later and wake up later. This is obviously very dependent on your situation as it may not be possible, for example, if you are in work or education – but if this is possible, it may be worth experimenting with this.

Some autistic and chronically ill individuals might struggle with their sleep due to dietary issues, such as if you have gastrointestinal symptoms. It can be worth exploring whether you need to eat earlier in the evening. You might also need to look at caffeine intake, though everyone reacts to this differently. Some might be told by professionals to reduce liquid intake in the evenings to help bladder-based symptoms.

If you are someone who needs to nap during the day, this can also affect your sleep at bedtimes. For some, these naps might need to happen before a certain point in the day or be at a consistent time of day, or you might need to go to bed slightly later to compensate. Some chronically ill people might be advised by their doctors to avoid naps to help them sleep at night, but this is not possible for everyone. Some people might find that if they do need to nap, keeping these to shorter periods of time can be helpful – such as keeping them to 20 minutes or half an hour.

Like a lot of management of everyday tasks as an autistic and chronically ill person, sleep can mean a lot of trial and error to find out what works. This can be frustrating and even exacerbate sleep issues – try to be kind to yourself about this, and if something doesn't work, know that you can try something else, even if it is something unconventional.

Public transport

Regardless of whether I am getting on a bus, train, the tube or even a tram, there are always multiple challenges for me to consider. For many non-disabled people, it's as simple as buying a ticket and getting on, but I'm always considering so many things about every single step: packing bags, buying tickets, getting to the station, getting to the platform/stop, the travel itself, getting off, getting to the place I was trying to get to... and I can't focus on the next part until I've completed the last bit.

There are multiple reasons for that – partly the way I experience anxiety and transitions as an autistic person, particularly about ending up at the wrong place or missing the train, as well as stress about social norms and doing the right thing whilst I'm out. In terms of my chronic illnesses, I also have to manage getting around the station, which is often inaccessible, and lifting luggage can also be difficult.

Some of the ways you might be able to help yourself navigate public transport include:

- Practising a journey if it is one you will be making regularly or need to ensure you make on time, such as before starting a new commute to work, school or university.

- Looking at maps of the journey beforehand and knowing what the route is. Additionally, many regional services have their own apps which show you timetables and routes.
- Knowing where your tickets or payments are, whether on your phone or in physical form. Some people prefer to have bus passes, Oyster cards or similar so they know that if their phone dies or their bank card doesn't work they can still use the transport they need.
- Using tools like Google Maps to look around the station or around the road the stop is on so you know what the environment will be like, whether there will be toilets or where the different platforms are. This can be particularly helpful if you are going to a station you haven't been to before, or have to do a change at another place you've never been to before.
- Having the essentials you need at hand in a cross-body bag or bumbag rather than in the bulk of your luggage so they are easy to access when using a mobility aid, when your luggage is put away or when you are amongst lots of people.
- Looking at whether the service has any passenger assistance you can use, such as helping you find your train or helping you to get yourself or your luggage onto the train.
- Booking priority seating or wheelchair seating that is near the front of the carriage and near luggage racks.
- Having sensory equipment with you such as headphones for if it is noisy, and stim toys to help you with regulation. It might also help to have an activity to distract you if the journey makes you anxious.
- Having snacks and a drink with you to make you feel more settled or if needed for condition management, such as water and salt which helps with POTS, sweets

to help with diabetes or chewing gum used as part of regulation techniques.

Aeroplanes can be difficult for many autistic people too, particularly with the anxiety of getting through security, airports being loud or the anxiety of the small space. As a chronically ill person, this might be increased with worries about getting medications or medical devices through, or symptoms being exacerbated by sitting for long periods, for example. Many airports have special assistance programs to help with this, and some have videos online of what the airport looks like or about their processes so you can understand them beforehand.

Driving

Not every chronically ill autistic person will legally be allowed to drive, and others may find that it is too inaccessible for them. However, some may find that they can learn and that it helps their independence in being able to travel.

Many disabled people can find that driving an automatic car can make it more accessible to them, because there are fewer actions to think about and it can be less tough on the body too. Others might find they need an adapted car, for example having hand controls, or steering wheel knobs which help you to turn the car more easily. There are also adaptations which can help you get in and out of the car, like swivel cushions or hoists.

Handling birthdays, festivities and holidays

There are a lot of reasons that autistic and chronically ill people might struggle with birthdays, festivities and holidays – whether that be Christmas, Diwali or Eid, as a few examples. When it comes to times like Christmas and New Year, you might not even be celebrating, but if you live in a country which celebrates this it tends to change how schools, workplaces and public spaces function, or is what their calendar of term times or holidays is based on.

You might struggle with:

- Changes in routine and structure – at school, work or home
- Changes to mealtimes or foods available
- Shops being busier or louder
- Expectations to react appropriately to gifts
- Lights, decorations or fireworks causing sensory overload
- More expectations to socialise, often in loud or unknown environments, which can exacerbate sensory overload, chronic pain, fatigue or brain fog, or other symptoms

There are some ways you might be able to support yourself during these periods, such as:

- Putting in your own structures where you can, like morning or night routines, time out to yourself, or mealtimes
- Having your safe foods available to you, and having spares!
- Doing online shopping or click and collect, or going to shops at off-peak times like in the evenings
- Talking to your family and friends about how you react differently to gifts, opening them away from others or messaging people after to thank them
- Having ear defenders, sunglasses or other sensory equipment available to support regulation and sensitivities
- Making sure to take time away from others when you need it, even if it is just a quick break or leaving early

Not everyone can enjoy festivities and holidays in the ways others can, and that can sometimes be upsetting to us. It can help to take the pressure off this and try and remember that it is okay if it isn't the best time of your life. You deserve to make occasions work for you, whatever that looks like. And if it is difficult, remember that it will end, and time moves on.

Using mobility aids

Mobility aids aren't helpful for everyone, but they can be for many people to support needs including reduction of pain or fatigue, making you steadier or less dizzy, giving you more mobility or supporting your independence.

There are a variety of mobility aids, from walking sticks to crutches, rollators to wheelchairs – and they are certainly not one size fits all. Many people also don't use only one type, and have different aids for different days depending on their needs.

Mobility aids are often seen as a 'last resort', but they can often be helpful long before someone has to start using them. They are also not a failure or you 'giving up', they are a tool to enable and support you to live your life to the best you can. You should not be ashamed to use one.

Which mobility aid you use as a chronically ill person may be impacted by your needs as an autistic person. For example, you might have proprioception issues which can make some harder to use than others, or touch sensitivity which may make certain handles difficult.

It's often recommended that you talk to a physiotherapist, occupational therapist or your doctor about starting to use a mobility aid. You may be eligible for funding for these, though unfortunately not everyone who needs them is. You can also go to mobility shops to try them out.

Whilst not exhaustive nor the same for everyone, a few situations that might show that a mobility aid could be helpful include:

- If you find yourself tired going around a supermarket
- If you struggle to stand in a queue, even for short periods
- If you fall down regularly
- If you experience pain when walking, even for short distances
- If you feel like you can't leave the house due to lack of support

I use a forearm crutch, but use a kind where the handle is tilted so that there is less pressure on my wrists. I used to use a walking stick, but there was too much pain in my wrists and it stopped providing the stability I needed. Everyone has different needs, so here are a few thoughts from others about what works for them:

> I use a walking stick in day-to-day life and have a manual wheelchair for longer days and holidays abroad. Having these mobility aids has given me freedom– it gives me independence, the ability to travel the world which I love to do, it helps me reduce my chronic illness symptoms (in particular pain and fatigue and reduces the post-exertion malaise after I have done the activity) and it makes me feel more confident. – **Meg**

> Adopting the approach of 'different aids for different days' is a really important part of me managing my chronic illnesses

and has made a huge positive impact in my ability to engage with day-to-day life. Choosing what mobility aid to use is always based off how I am feeling and what I need to do that day. I use a combination of a walking stick, manual wheelchair and powerchair dependent on the location, my symptoms and what feels the m ost beneficial in the moment.

If using my powerchair, I tend to wear noise cancelling headphones as the noise that the motor makes is an added sensory input that I find quite tricky, especially given that when I normally use my powerchair it's during a long day that has other sensory stimulation associated with it. My walking stick, as well as providing me with more stability when walking, also helps with my proprioception; having something outside of my body that I can hold, marking where I am in an environment is really useful. – **Amber**

I used to use medical crutches and knee supporters the first few years after my leg surgery. But it impacted my life quality in a bad way. My pain was reduced but using crutches made it harder for me to be mobile (my country is a country with less to no accessibility, especially for disabled people – especially for us who don't have the choice to not be working. Hectic activities are even harder with this condition).

Now I use muscle tapes/kinesio tapes to support myself walking and doing heavier activities, though the tapes irritate my skin, cause discomfort and scars, I feel the freest mobility-wise when using tapes. – **MS**

I use crutches inside and a wheelchair outside. It gives me a lot of independence and helps massively with preventing swings in blood glucose, because I am not in as much pain (so fewer high blood glucose levels) and not walking (so fewer low blood glucose levels). It also gives me freedom to do things as and when I feel like, not when others are available or want to do it. – **Elli**

It is really hard to find the right one especially when the social norm is not to use them. I was lucky to have a physio who supported me to find crutches and then reluctantly supported me to get a chair but you should be able to access them more easily. You should know that mobility aids shouldn't cause you pain, like wrist pain through crutches. Sometimes they are itchy or cause sensory discomfort from the sounds coming from them. Your mobility aid shouldn't be at the cost of your sensory comfort either. – **Alice**

KEY TAKEAWAYS FROM THIS CHAPTER

- You aren't lazy for using shortcuts, equipment, aids or 'hacks' that make your life easier and more accessible to you.
- You aren't a failure for needing support to do tasks or activities that others can do more easily, or not being able to shower every day.
- Sometimes there are specific disability aids that can help you do tasks, other times there are ways to adapt life with everyday items or everyday ideas.

3

Sensory needs

Sometimes I feel like I am my own caretaker. Like – my body has all these needs and my brain is the one making sure it's safe and healthy and happy. I'm really good at designing systems and optimising things, and I put that talent towards taking care of my body. It helps me to think this way because I can be gentler with myself. – **Emily**

A huge part of autism is based around sensory needs and sensory differences, with it being a focal point of what many struggle with or have to find ways to adjust their life to. For many, there are lots of ways we can regulate and support these needs to make them less of a difficulty and more just a part of who we are, but this is often complex and not simple to unpick and understand.

When you are chronically ill, you might also experience some sensory needs as a part of your condition. For example, your response to pain can often surround how it feels, or you might not be able to handle certain smells or sounds when you are also struggling with pain or fatigue.

I have found that being both autistic and chronically ill means there is a lot of crossover between some of these different needs and it is where my experience of being multiple disabled is most prominent. In this chapter, we will explore a large range of these differences and how being both autistic and chronically ill can impact this, what you can do to learn about your own needs, and some ways to manage them and support sensory regulation.

An introduction to sensory needs

Before we can think about specific senses or consider how you might need to regulate yourself, we must have an understanding of how sensory needs and differences work.

In this chapter I will refer to sensory needs and sensory differences rather than sensory issues, for the reason that they are so variable in everyone. These terms can be contentious because our sensory needs can have detrimental impacts on our lives in a way that is not just produced by society (in comparison, for example, to communication differences being seen as a deficit by society that is manufactured by allistics; sensory needs are partially internal).

Sensory processing has been defined as how the body receives, analyses and then responds to the signals received from the surrounding environment.[1] Everyone experiences sensory processing and will have individual sensory needs, but there are fundamental differences in the neurology of autistic people which change our reactions to stimuli. In allistic people, or individuals without sensory processing difficulties, it is easier to tune out or process sensory input, meaning it is often received, but either not responded to, or can be enjoyed in a way an autistic person might not experience.

When we discuss sensory processing, it can be split into a number of different forms of how we register and respond to sensory inputs.[2] These include:

- Sensory registration – being hyposensitive to sensory stimuli, being slower to detect it

- Sensory sensitivity – being hypersensitive to sensory stimuli, being quicker to detect it
- Sensory seeking – actively looking for sensory stimuli
- Sensory aversion – actively avoiding sensory stimuli

Often, these will come in pairs – if you are hypersensitive to a stimuli, you are likely to avoid it, whereas if you are hyposensitive, you are more likely to seek it out. However, this is not an exact science, and can depend on the individual stimuli and your thresholds for them.

It also doesn't mean you will react to a stimulus the exact same way every time you encounter it – it might depend on the physical environment you are in, or whether you are already experiencing sensory overload, for example.

When you add chronic illness to the mix, this will also change the way you react to stimuli or the way you have to cope with sensory inputs, which may sometimes contrast or clash with that which you experience as an autistic person. Your symptoms like pain may increase your sensory sensitivity as you are already dealing with internal sensory input that may be significantly heightened in contrast to your non-chronically ill peers, for example. Throughout this chapter we will discuss some of these situations, such as dealing with uncomfortable medical equipment, or making stimming behaviours accessible to you.

Working with healthcare professionals and receiving healthcare can often be impacted by sensory needs. We discussed communication with professionals in more depth in Chapter 1, and it can help to incorporate discussions of any sensory needs into this. You may want to build a sensory profile, or use a sensory assessment if you have one done by professionals, to support your needs.

Sensory profiles

Sensory profiles are sometimes called sensory checklists or sensory reports. They detail your sensory needs and help you to understand your sensory system. Everyone's sensory needs and sensory system are unique to them, even those of two people who are both autistic and have the same chronic illness.

You could go through this chapter building your own sensory profile. Use each subheading to consider:

- How you experience hypersensitivity or hyposensitivity – many people find that they experience both in different ways for each sense
- What sort of sensory input you find overstimulating or understimulating
- Support aids you can use to regulate these forms of sensory input
- How you can prevent meltdowns/shutdowns and how you can plan for when these do occur
- How your chronic illness impacts your sensory needs and how you can support this

You could then also continue to consider this in the other chapters. For example, if you are reading Chapter 5, Education and employment, you could add a section on your profile about support you need to put in place in those settings.

Some people will create a sensory profile alongside an occupational therapist or other professional. These can be very helpful, but even if you already have one, you might find it helpful to go through this chapter considering how your chronic illness may also have an effect, as a standard assessment won't include this. Professional assessments are also sometimes written in deficits-based language, so you may find you want to create yourself something more neurodivergence affirming.

Sensory oversensitivity[3]

Many autistic people will find that they are hypersensitive when it comes to many of their senses, often particularly those we experience externally (sound, taste, touch, smell, sight), though many also find some hypersensitivity to the internal senses (interoception, vestibular and proprioception). You might particularly struggle with the latter as a chronically ill person, as your chronic symptoms are likely to impact these.

Sometimes sensory sensitivity can cause not only mental distress and overwhelm, but physical pain too. It can also be very exhausting.

When you are also chronically ill, your sensory sensitivity might increase your symptoms like pain or fatigue from having to process them.

Sound
Sound can often be overwhelming for autistic people in a number of ways, such as:

- Volume
- Pitch or tone
- Repetitiveness
- Unexpectedness
- Layers of noises

For example, some autistic people will find noises such as fireworks difficult because they are not only loud but also unexpected, and therefore uncontrollable by the individual.

You might find that there are specific noises that trigger you, or you might more generally find it difficult to be in a noisy environment because there are too many noises (such as a busy supermarket) or it simply is too loud.

Sound sensitivity might also mean you find it more difficult to have conversations when in a noisy environment as you cannot process everything at once.

Meg talked about their difficulties with noise sensitivity, saying:

I struggle the most with sounds – unexpected sounds like doors slamming or people yelling when I am not anticipating it. I find it difficult to focus on conversations when there are unexpected sounds in the background as I cannot cut them out.

On the other hand, silence is incredibly uncomfortable for me too, and I cannot work without music or videos playing in the background. I manage this by either wearing earphones or noise cancelling headphones while completing tasks. The louder an atmosphere is, the more fatigued I will feel by trying to manage it, which can cause a chronic illness flare to occur. – **Meg**

Many autistic people also experience hyperacusis and misophonia.

Hyperacusis refers to experiencing sounds in an intrusive and uncomfortable way, and can often include hearing everyday sounds at a higher volume. For example, many autistic people find they can hear sounds from much further away or hear sounds that others can't, like hearing electricity.

Misophonia refers to decreased tolerance to sounds which can cause anger, irritation or stress. This is often with repetitive sounds or those made by other human beings, like noises from eating, lip-smacking or tapping. This can be quite distressing for individuals who experience it.

Some ways that might help you to deal with overwhelm from sound can be:

- Using ear defenders, earplugs or noise cancelling headphones
- Eating away from other people
- Taking time out of events or places that are overwhelming (some places may have a quiet space or you may want to request one)
- Making sure you decompress after being in a noisy environment
- Use technology such as self-checkouts to reduce needing to process talking to someone

Lauren is an autistic and ADHD person who has recently become chronically ill due to long Covid. They explained the crossover of their autistic traits and chronic symptoms when it comes to noise:

> A lot of my sensory needs overlap with what causes exhaustion due to long Covid. Even if I don't realise it, I find that lots of different conversations occurring at once is very overwhelming and tiring, especially since I have brain fog and issues with auditory processing. This means that if I have to endure this for a long time, I can become really fatigued or have headaches. – **Lauren**

Smell

Smells can also be difficult for autistic people, particularly because there are not many ways to block them out with self-management tools unlike some of the other senses. Smells cannot be gotten away from even when we are sleeping. Like the other senses, we are particularly likely to be hypersensitive to smell, and often may be able to smell something that others can't.

For many chronically ill people who struggle with nausea, smells can be a particularly difficult sense to deal with.

Smells may be difficult because they are too intense, strong, unpleasant, sharp or synthetic, for example. It may also be more difficult when multiple smells are combined at once.

A few ways you might be able to deal with overwhelm from smell can be:

- Buying unscented cleaning products or always buying the same ones
- Chewing gum to help nausea and distract from the smell
- Avoiding perfume, or asking people not to wear it when they are around you

Taste

We are going to talk about eating and drinking as a chronically ill autistic person later in this chapter in more detail. However, many of us have specific hypersensitivities to taste itself, as well as texture and other issues with food.

There are four main taste areas on the tongue – sweet, salty, bitter and sour. Some autistic people might have particular sensitivity to just one of these areas, or to multiple, or to all of them at varying degrees.

Some autistic people will limit themselves to a very bland diet because of oversensitivity to taste. There isn't anything inherently wrong with this, but you may want to consult with doctors about any needs for supplements or vitamins. Avoidant restrictive food intake disorder (ARFID) is also very common in autistic individuals.

Texture is also a big part of taste oversensitivity for many. This can change how the taste of food is processed as it can change the strength or aroma.

Touch

Whilst being autistic can mean touch is difficult, many methods of managing chronic illness or dealing with healthcare professionals can involve it. A few ways that touch may be difficult for those who are hypersensitive may include:

- Being touched by someone causing pain or discomfort
- Struggling with washing yourself
- Not liking some clothing textures or finding labels itchy or painful
- Struggling with having bandages or plasters on, or with using gels or creams

Sometimes difficulties with touch are around touching the material or formula of the object, whereas in other situations it is more about something or someone touching you.

Some ways you can try to reduce overstimulation and difficulties from touch might include:

- Using a glove, sponge or mitt to apply gels or creams instead of using your fingers, or having someone else apply it if that is easier
- Working with healthcare professionals to understand when they will touch you and how, or work out if it is necessary
- Cut out labels in clothing and wear textures you prefer – this might include not wearing hospital clothing/gowns as a reasonable adjustment (if allowed under infection rules)
- Using aids to help you wash such as shampoo caps
- Using weighted blankets or lap pads for grounding, if you like deep pressure but not light touch
- Asking people to ask permission before hugging you or touching you

Sight

It is very common for autistic people to struggle with sight and vision in some way, as it can take a lot of processing when in outside environments. When you are chronically ill, this may be combined with nausea or migraines around difficult light levels, for example.

Some of the ways that autistic and chronically ill people might struggle with sight include:

- Being sensitive to light or finding it painful
- Struggling to take in everything around you, which could mean bumping into things
- Vision being distorted or things moving around
- Struggling with lights flickering that others might not notice
- Not liking bright colours
- Needing to squint to focus
- Struggling to look at screens

I have a real sensitivity to light, I need very specific levels and places for light. And I'm very very uncomfortable with full dark. So my house is full of night lights, and also floor lamps that are connected to remote controls. I mounted the remote controls where the regular light switch would be, so whenever I walk into a room I can immediately adjust the lighting to how I want it that moment. This is important especially when I'm in a lot of pain so I don't have to move around to the different lamps. – **Emily**

Some ways that you might be able to support hypersensitivity when it comes to sight and light include:

- Wearing sunglasses, or blue-light glasses when looking at screens
- Using pastel colours for walls rather than bright colours
- Having blackout curtains and non-fluorescent lighting
- Working at a desk that is against a blank wall
- Not having clutter around

Many healthcare environments are very brightly or badly lit, which could cause particular challenges as an autistic and chronically ill person who is likely to need to use them often. You might need to consider how you could support this need whilst navigating these environments, whether that be with sunglasses or a hat, or making sure that you get lots of rest immediately afterwards.

Interoception

We already talked about interoception in Chapter 1 in terms of its impacts on communicating with healthcare professionals, but it can also have a huge impact when it comes to understanding your sensory needs and how these work in relation to your chronic illnesses.

Many autistic people are more prominently hyposensitive to their needs around interoception, but you can also have hypersensitivities to this too.

Hypersensitivity when it comes to interoception can look like:

- Being hyper-aware of or overwhelmed by your body signals
- Feeling like you need the toilet more often
- Feeling full very quickly or feeling nauseous after drinking water
- Being hyper-aware of pain
- Being distracted by your heartbeat

This can be very difficult for chronically ill people because there is so much happening within our bodies, a lot of it that we might want to try and distract ourselves from or that we might need to try and self-manage. Our symptoms being amplified to the point we cannot focus on anything else can be extremely difficult. As someone with POTS, being constantly aware of and distracted by my heartbeat is hard when it is normally going at a much faster than normal pace.

Adam is an autistic and ADHD person who has a colostomy and chronic pain due to bowel prolapses and chronic constipation. He said:

> When I am in pain, nothing else matters, and it becomes completely consuming, so even the slightest thing can send me into overload. Pain plus fatigue also burns me out very quickly and I become very insular and isolated because I simply cannot cope with anything else. I also have formed new stims such as playing with my stoma bag and massaging my stomach as a form of emotional detachment. – **Adam**

Vestibular

The vestibular sense refers to our sense of movement and balance; it is connected to our head and inner ears moving. This is the sense that can quite often make us struggle with motion sickness, and there are some disorders that are specific to it.

Autistic and chronically ill people might struggle with the vestibular sense in ways such as:

- Feeling sick whilst travelling
- Avoiding being off the ground and feeling dizzy easily
- Not being able to control movements easily
- Struggling to stop and start when moving

Some of the ways that you might be able to support hypersensitivity to the vestibular sense could include:

- Using weighted objects to feel more centred
- Controlling vestibular input through choice movement, such as (but not limited to):
  - Swings
  - Yoga
  - Rocking chairs
- Breaking movements down into smaller steps

Proprioception

Proprioception is our sense of where our bodies are in relation to space, including how we are moving our body parts. Although autistic people may struggle with this sense independent of any other condition, dyspraxia or developmental coordination disorder (DCD) is also a common co-occurring condition with autism.

Some of the ways you might be hypersensitive to this sense are:

- Struggling with activities like doing your shoelaces or doing up buttons, or other fine-motor activities
- Putting too much pressure on things or breaking things
- Struggling with standing up and preferring to sit down
- Avoiding tight clothes
- Bumping into furniture
- Slumping and struggling to sit up straight

Ways you can support hypersensitivity to proprioception include:

- Using weighted items or deep pressure therapy to regulate
- Using chew jewellery or fidgets to feel more centred
- You may prefer chairs and furniture which have arms
- Wearing looser clothing

Overstimulation, meltdowns and shutdowns[4]

If you become overstimulated or overwhelmed, you may experience a meltdown or shutdown when everything builds up and becomes too much for your system to cope with. There are lots of possible causes for both of these, which could include:

- Changes to routines or structures
- Sensory overload
- Social situations becoming too much

Chey told me about how masking impacts overstimulation:

I make sure I will have sleep and rest time after social events (including work) as I struggle with fatigue due to masking. I fold and layer a weighted blanket so that its combined weight is more over my torso, hips and feet, where I often get pain.

I have a keyring, a magnet and a small carabiner clip on my car keys, which are kept in my right trouser pocket so that I can fidget/stim relatively unnoticed.

I use vocal (humming) stims to help reduce the intensity or pressure of a situation that I don't like. If I'm burnt out I become non-verbal, but have vocal hums/stims to communicate with my husband. – **Chey**

Meltdowns tend to include a lack of control over your behaviour, whether that be through verbal or physical means – the former including but not limited to crying or shouting, and the latter rocking or kicking. These are often misunderstood as 'temper tantrums', particularly in younger people.

Shutdowns, though still happening when someone is overwhelmed or overstimulated, are a different response – when someone withdraws themselves and may not be able to engage in communication or might not be able to physically move. It is not uncommon for autistic people to have a meltdown that then becomes a shutdown due to the intensity of the situation.

When you are chronically ill, meltdowns can be extremely difficult to handle as they are very physically demanding on the body. You might find that they cause you additional pain or fatigue, for example, and you need to rest more following them.

You may find it helpful to prepare for these situations and have a plan with those who support you in order to minimise the possible damage of having a meltdown or shutdown. Here are some questions that you may want to consider:

- What items are helpful to use during a meltdown or shutdown? For example, ear defenders, fidget toys or comfort items?
- Do you need to be spoken to during a meltdown or shutdown, and how can you be supported to communicate? For example, will you prefer to communicate through written means?
- Are there any objects or supports that can help you minimise exacerbating chronic symptoms? For example, do you need cushions around you, or need to put on joint supports?
- Do you want someone to stay with you to help, or would you prefer to be alone?

It may also be helpful to consider ways in which you can prevent these situations from occurring in the first place. Ways you can begin to do this could include:

- Try to identify what tends to trigger you. You might find that you have them in very specific places, or are more likely to have a meltdown in one but a shutdown in another, for example.
- Work out what can help you to calm down before you are pushed into meltdown or shutdown. For example, do you need to shorten social time, find a quiet space or use sensory aids?
- If there is going to be a change to the plan or routine, how can you minimise the impact of this? For example, do you need a timetable, or to talk through the change with someone?

Harriet told me about her experience of meltdowns and how they relate to her PCOS:

I experience lower back and abdomen pain with ovulation, and this coincides with increased sensitivity to light and sound. As such, when I experience this pain I find that meltdowns are triggered much more quickly by things such as bright spaces or background noise. I am also more irritable during these periods, and so find the best thing to do is to maintain my accommodations (glasses, earbuds) when I need to go out but otherwise to insulate myself and remain in my room, where I can control sensory input to a higher degree. Stimming is useful to an extent but I find that when I am in pain already it is less effective, especially because the types of stim I can conduct in public (tapping, rotating ring around finger) are less calming than the bigger stims (rocking, hair pulling) I can conduct in private. As such, staying in my room seems to be the most effective way of managing my needs at this time, no matter how isolating. – **Harriet**

Sensory hyposensitivity

Being hyposensitive to your senses often leads to autistic people becoming 'sensory seekers', making them look for more sensory input in order to feel balanced and regulated within themselves. This can occur with all eight of our different senses, and every single autistic person will experience this in different ways and on varying scales.

An autistic person being hypersensitive to one of the senses does not mean they cannot also be hyposensitive to that sense in other ways, but they are likely to be searching for it in ways different to the kinds they avoid.

Sound

Being hyposensitive to sound as an autistic person can sometimes mean simply not acknowledging all sounds, or it may mean sensory seeking and looking for more auditory input.

If you are someone who struggles to acknowledge sound then you might prefer to have visual supports rather than auditory ones. For example, having visual timetables, or being given visual instructions, to make sure that you process these types of information.

When it comes to seeking auditory input, you might for example want to be in noisy places, or always be listening to music (many sensory seek with a preferred genre, or with a certain instrument in).

Many autistic people enjoy concerts for this reason. If you are chronically ill, concerts can be very tiring, cause pain or make symptoms like dizziness worse. You might find them easier to access with use of a mobility aid, through seated tickets and through asking for accommodations such as not having to queue up.

Smell

Being hyposensitive to smells can manifest in multiple ways. Some autistic people don't pick up on certain smells or won't be able to differentiate between different ones. They might also seek out more smells, for example enjoying cooking or liking having candles around them.

Some autistic and chronically ill sensory seekers might find that although they want more input in this way, it might make them nauseous or dizzy. It can be trial and error to work out which smells cause these issues, and what can be done instead. You may find that stronger essential oils or perfumes can cause issues where others might not.

Taste

Autistic people who are hyposensitive to tastes may search out foods that are spicy, sour or strong, or perhaps those that have thick or varying textures. They might want more salt or condiments on their food.

Some may also over-eat due to this searching out of certain flavours, textures or mouth feelings. This is discussed later on in the chapter.

When you are chronically ill, eating can often come with other complications. These are also discussed later in the chapter.

Some autistic people may also experience pica, which is a condition that causes someone to eat items that aren't edible, like grass, wood or sponges, for example.

Touch

Being hyposensitive to touch can mean many different things for autistic people. Some of the ways of showing hyposensitivity to touch can include:

- Wanting lots of deep pressure, for example through tight hugs or use of a weighted blanket
- Having a much higher pain threshold than others
- Seeking out different textures, with anything from soft blankets to grass or smooth metal
- Not feeling hot temperatures until they are burning
- Wanting to chew things often
- Rubbing your arms or legs against things

There are a variety of things that you can do to support these needs. You might like to have a box of things with different textures that you can feel, such as different fabrics and fidget toys. Similarly, you might like to have something that you can chew available, like chewing gum or stim toys made for chewing.

Sometimes this can combine with symptoms of chronic illnesses as these needs may clash. For example, some people with chronic pain may find deep pressure exacerbates this. Some chronically ill people also struggle to regulate temperature, and so if you are touch hyposensitive, you might further struggle to know when you need to do something to change your temperature.

Sight
Sight hyposensitivity can show up in different ways. For some, it will be about what they physically see – having blurred peripheral vision, or struggling with depth perception. For others, it will be more about how they take sights in, for example struggling to see patterns or small details.

Interoception
Many autistic people struggle with being hyposensitive to interoception. This includes:

- Not knowing when you are hungry or thirsty
- Not realising you need the bathroom
- Not being aware of pain or other bodily sensations

One of my worst issues with interoception is with hydration. Ever since I was a child I've always forgotten to drink anything – it just doesn't come into my head. The way I now combat this is through having big bottles with straws, so I don't have to fill them up very often and I'm more likely to reach for them if they're next to my laptop or on my bedside table, for example. There are also bottles available which have prompts on the side to encourage your water intake throughout the day.

You might find that your experience is similar to this, possibly with something different like eating or remembering to go to the toilet.

This can be particularly problematic when you are chronically ill, as a lot of management for many chronic illnesses can include making sure you are hydrated, eating in specific ways or managing your bladder and bowel movements.

Some of the ways I try to balance my needs as a chronically ill person with my issues with interoception include:

- Visual prompts to eat, drink or go to the toilet, such as reminders on my phone or smartwatch, or sticky notes in front of my laptop
- Scheduling in my meals, and making sure not to put meetings over lunchtimes
- Having snacks and water easily available in my workspace in case I don't remember until I get dizzy or over-hungry
- Going to the toilet and filling my water bottle between meetings (which you could also schedule!)
- Habit stacking: doing these things when you do something else that is a part of your routine already

There are many apps you can use to schedule and provide visual reminders, such as Tiimo.

Another issue you might find if you struggle with interoception is that you struggle to regulate your temperature. For example, many of us will think we are cold even in the summer, and might overheat ourselves because of it. If you also have a chronic illness that makes temperature regulation a struggle – whether heat intolerance, or being colder than you should be – this might be even harder.

Dylan is an autistic person with a variety of chronic illnesses including EDS, Sjogren's syndrome, fibromyalgia and hypogonadism caused by premature ovarian failure. They said:

> Sensory sensitivity from autism/ADHD plus central nervous sensitisation from fibromyalgia equals a special kind of hell. It can be hard to tell the two apart sometimes. When my subjective experience of temperature fluctuates rapidly, going from hot flashes to chills in a mild room within minutes, is that autism or fibromyalgia (or both?). – **Dylan**

In the cold, if you use a wheelchair a blanket may be helpful as you will not be moving your body and may become colder. In colder weather, warm drinks can help, and hand warmers may be helpful to provide a smaller amount of extra warmth. Try not to have scaldingly hot showers or baths as a way to warm up, as this may make you hot too quickly and exacerbate symptoms.

If you are heat intolerant, using a fan or spraying yourself with water consistently when it is hot outside may be helpful, even if you don't feel hot in that moment due to interoception difficulties. You may also need to put in more reminders to drink water or eat salty snacks, for example. Eating smaller, lighter meals multiple times a day can help your system, rather than eating a smaller number of large meals. You should also keep curtains and windows shut.

You might find that wearing multiple lighter layers of clothing is better than wearing thicker clothing as you can reduce or increase temperature more slowly.

If you struggle to recognise when you are too hot or cold, you may want to be aware of symptoms that you might feel if the temperature is becoming problematic so you can know what to do next. For example, getting dizzy when hot, or shivering when cold.

Vestibular

Those who are hyposensitive to their vestibular (balance) sense are more likely to engage in stimming like rocking, spinning or swinging. Later in the chapter we will discuss how to make this accessible to you as a chronically ill person if these sorts of actions will exacerbate your symptoms such as dizziness or vertigo.

Some who are hyposensitive to this sense may also be clumsy or lose balance often. For chronically ill autistic people, it can be difficult to tell whether this comes from this hyposensitivity or from symptoms of their chronic illness.

Proprioception

Being hyposensitive to proprioceptive input (awareness of your body in space) can manifest in multiple different ways:

- Struggling to navigate around and often bumping into doorways, people or obstacles
- Standing too close to people or struggling to judge where to stand
- Slouching or preferring to lean into people
- Dropping things or having a weak grasp
- Walking on your toes or W-sitting on the floor (when you sit with knees bent and feet positioned away from your hips, so it looks like a W)

Being both autistic and hypermobile, for example, can mean that your hyposensitivity to proprioceptive input affects your body in a physical manner. For example, slouching may hurt your back or cause 'coat-hanger' pain, whilst walking on your toes can cause your joints to become tighter.

There are some ways that you can support hyposensitivity to proprioception, although many recommendations for this are often not those which all chronically ill individuals can partake in, like bouncing on a trampoline or doing heavy lifting. Here are some that you may be able to do:

- Using weighted blankets or lap pads
- Stretching resistance bands on your arms or legs
- Placing your furniture along the edges or in corners of rooms to make navigation easier
- Having chairs with arms available

What is stimming?

'Stimming' is a term short for self-stimulatory behaviours, which we do as part of sensory regulation. This could be to calm ourselves down when overstimulated, or to cause more stimulation when we are understimulated.

Sometimes stimming may be done unconsciously without us realising we are doing it, when stressed or excited for example, whereas sometimes it may be a choice done to try and prevent dysregulation before it occurs.

There are hundreds of ways to stim, but here are a few examples:

- Repetitive physical actions such as flapping your hands, tapping, pacing or spinning around

- Use of fidget/sensory toys, such as tangles, stress balls or pop-its
- Use of external stimuli such as listening to loud music, listening to white or brown noise, chewing food or watching television
- Auditory stimming, such as humming or echolalia (repetition of noises, phrases, words, sentences or songs)
- Visual stimming, such as blinking, lining things up or staring at something like a light

Some stims can be harmful to the individual or be a self-harm behaviour. In these cases, you may need support from a professional such as a psychologist. However, many stims are not harmful and are just an important part of self-regulation.

> I am a massive sensory seeker of deep pressure and hugs. I find it helps my joints feel better and my body feel more normal. It helps reduce my stress, which makes my head feel better too.
>
> My sensory issues really affect my mobility. My balance and walking are already affected by the IIH [idiopathic intracranial hypertension] and hypermobility. Poor proprioception and vestibular senses just add more complication. I am unbelievably uncoordinated and movement takes so much effort that I fatigue really easily. This has led to me being quite stationary, which has unfortunately impacted my health a lot.
>
> I stim a lot and always have. My body is always moving. Sometimes, I've found that it impacts me later though, as I'll feel achy if I've overdone it. – **Eli**

Stimming and chronic illness – being safe

When you are a chronically ill autistic person, stimming can become a little bit more complicated. You may find that there are certain stims you do that exacerbate your chronic illness symptoms which you might have to avoid or adapt.

I need to physically stim to self-regulate. Unfortunately, sometimes this is hard when I'm particularly fatigued and/or in pain in relevant places, such as finding it hard to lift my arms, or stand. It often feels like my body needs two separate, opposing things – rest, in stillness and without further exerting myself, and movement. In these cases, I have to stim with lighter and less strenuous movements in order to continue self-regulating, something that is essential to my wellbeing. – **Dan**

For example, I used to like to spin around repetitively as one of my favourite stims, but as my POTS has increased and I struggled more with dizziness, I can't do this. To satisfy this stim, I have replaced it with moving my arms in circles or rocking back and forth which are also stims that work with the vestibular sense.

You might also need to be more careful with stims that use your joints if these are unstable and you experience dislocations or subluxations. For some people, kinesiology tape or joint splints/supports can mean that this is accessible, but others might find that it is not something they can do.

You may also find that stimming causes you to be more fatigued. You might have to experiment with different types of stims to find a balance: those which satisfy the need for regulation but that do not exacerbate your symptoms and make life more difficult to navigate.

The sensory need and rest cycle

One issue I have found with my sensory needs is the fact that I need to rest more than your average person due to my chronic illnesses, but this makes me massively understimulated.

Some people tell autistic individuals that if they are burnt out or struggling that they might need to rest but this might need to be in a more 'active' way in order to combat understimulation, for example reading a book, going for a walk or going to the cinema.

For me as a chronically ill person, my rest can't look like that because I often can't even hold a book when I am at that point, but listening to music or watching a TV show doesn't necessarily fill in the stimulation need.

Because of this, I often experience a cycle:

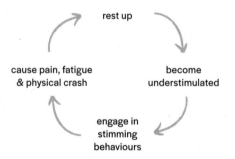

This cycle can be extremely tiring and difficult to combat. In order to think about how we can start to try and deal with this issue, let's consider some accessible stimming ideas.

Accessible stimming

Not all stims will be accessible for all disabled people, much like with other activities. You might need to adapt something in order to receive the same sensory feedback in an accessible manner.

For example:

- Instead of tapping your fingers, tapping a pen may put less pressure on the finger joints
- Using a weighted lap pad instead of a blanket so you can lift it
- Wearing blue light glasses or sunglasses to prevent damage or eye strain

When it comes to accessible stimming, another thing you may need to adapt to is your energy levels and fatigue. Although everyone will have different versions of what takes up their energy, a few low energy stims could include:

- Listening to music
- Using a fidget toy
- Using stim apps such as Heat Pad or Antistress
- Chewing gum or sucking sour sweets
- Using a colour-changing light or projection

Dealing with uncomfortable medical equipment or treatments

One of the main ways I have found the crossover of my sensory needs and chronic illnesses difficult has been when I have needed to use certain types of medical equipment. For me, this has mainly included joint splints and supports, but it could also include (but is not limited to):

- Feeding tubes, PICC (peripherally inserted central catheter) lines or other central lines
- TENS machines (see below)
- Dressings and creams
- Orthotics or prosthetics
- Catheters

Any of this sort of equipment can cause sensory difficulties, whether it's because it's painful, itchy, uncomfortable or just annoying.

When it comes to splints and supports, I have found that the best way to work with them is to try them out for short periods when I first get them to try and get used to the fabric and the metal that is often in them. Where some are for the purpose of reducing pain, others are there to try and put your joints back in their 'correct' places which can be really difficult. I make sure that the other clothes I am wearing at the time are super comfortable and I also try to reduce or regulate any other sensory input coming in to try and prevent overstimulation.

I find creams or gels very difficult due to the texture of them and not liking my skin being massaged in the way they often need. It can help to apply these with my palms or wrists instead of with my fingers, or apply them with gloves on.

Catheters, whether they are temporary or permanent, can be very uncomfortable. Wearing loose clothing or trying different accessories for them can support you when they are in. You should make sure to use new supplies and make sure you are aware of any problems or signs of infection.

TENS machines are used for pain – TENS stands for transcutaneous electrical nerve stimulation and they send mild currents to the skin. Not everyone with be comfortable with this, particularly if it provides too much sensory discomfort, so you might find it helpful to distract yourself or use other sensory regulation whilst you are using a TENS machine. Sometimes a physiotherapist or pain specialist might show you how to use one or loan you one if it seems like it may be helpful. They are not safe for everyone to use, so it can be worth checking with a professional.

There is more discussion about feeding tubes in the 'Eating and drinking' section at the end of the chapter.

> One of my treatments is to inject medication fortnightly. Due to my autism, I have a resistance inside my own head to it even though I know it is the right thing to do. Therefore, I often need support to push past that. – **Becky**

> I wear an insulin pump and continuous glucose monitor (CGM) which can be sensory hell. Sometimes I have to change my site or sensor several times in one day to make it feel 'right' (sites are meant to be changed every two days, sensor every seven). I can't tell if my blood glucose is high or low because my interoception is terrible, so I have fully funded CGM on the NHS and I panic if I can't check what my blood glucose is (extremely unusual when I got it in 2009, less so now). – **Elli**

Internal feelings or symptoms and their part in sensory needs

There will always be irony to me in the way that my own body provides some of my sensory difficulties – the crossover of my conditions is very inconvenient in this way!

Sometimes my pain is not only painful in that part of my body, but the way it makes me feel nauseous, unbalanced or overstimulated can be extremely difficult and make me feel like I need to almost crawl out of my own body to get rid of it. It can lead to meltdowns and shutdowns in its own right, even before any of the external stimuli that also cause those feelings.

This is similar with dizziness and heart palpitations, as they feel so odd and make me feel off-centre in my own body.

Dislocations or subluxations (partial dislocations) may also be extremely difficult on a sensory level, particularly if you are someone who has to wait for them to relocate or they happen constantly.

Although not foolproof, some of the ways I try to soothe from these feelings and how they make me feel in my own body are:

- Using heat or cold:
  I use ice packs or electric heating pads interchangeably depending on how I feel, but both of these make me feel like I have more control over how my body feels. Heat can soothe pain whereas cold can change how adrenalised I feel or make me regulate my temperature better.
- Listening to music:
  I have specific artists and playlists that can distract or soothe me. Some of these will be calmer, but sometimes I need something really upbeat or loud to make me focus on the pain less.
- Getting my hair off my face and putting on comfortable clothes or pyjamas:
  This might sound trivial but when I'm already struggling with the internal natures of my body, things externally touching me such as these can send me right into overload. I make sure that there isn't any uncomfortable fabric, labels or hair tickling me to try and reduce that overload.
- Using deep pressure:
  Deep pressure certainly isn't helpful for everyone – for some people it may make their pain worse or they might find they still experience sensory overload from it. However, I like to use a weighted blanket or have very

firm hugs from someone as I can focus on that feeling instead and because it is all one firm feeling it isn't lots of stimulation. Remember, if you are buying a weighted blanket, it should never be over 10 percent of your body weight.

- Eating or drinking something that gives sensory feedback:
  Some examples of foods or drinks that might give you sensory feedback to focus on might be salt and vinegar crisps, thick milkshakes, sour or hard boiled sweets and crunchy carrot sticks. Here you are looking for something that is distracting and/or satisfying in a sensory way.
- Having colourful lights:
  I have a few different lamps that help my sensory needs by flashing or transitioning through different colours. Although this one is probably the least effective of the list, it helps to add another level of sensory support and gives me something different to focus on which I think is helpful.

You might find that a number of these ideas help you, or they might not at all – everyone is totally different when it comes to sensory needs and this is particularly true when you are in a body that is reacting in ways that it doesn't for most people because you have to learn how to best cope with every combination.

It might be that you need to experiment with different forms of sensory supports. You might come across some that you immediately recoil from or that simply don't do anything for you, and others might have an instant pull. Try out a few different things and try them in combination, too!

Some aspects of certain chronic illnesses might provide more specific sensory discomfort. For example, having a stoma or ostomy and having to empty a stoma bag, or having to administer insulin or testing blood sugar levels for some diabetic people.

Diabetes UK have resources about making injecting insulin more comfortable, such as using injection aids or numbing the area with ice first.[5] Some might find it helpful to be distracted or to have someone else do it for them.

When it comes to testing blood sugars, finger pricking is common though others use glucose monitors such as the FreeStyle Libre. The former can be uncomfortable, but it can help to have warm hands and switch which finger you use regularly, and there are different sizes of device to make it more comfortable.

Crohn's & Colitis UK have information about living with a stoma.[6] It might change how you eat, live and exercise amongst other things. You might find sensory discomfort with changing and emptying your stoma bag or having sore skin. The latter can be due to needing to change it, and there are types of wipes and powders which can help this. You might find it helpful to change your bag more regularly to prevent leaks and make yourself more comfortable.

Having periods

For any autistic person who has periods, they tend to be quite difficult on a sensory level – they change a lot of your body sensations as well as having to deal with the difficulty of the bleeding itself, changing period products and dealing with issues like cramps.

When you add chronic illness to this, you may also be dealing with issues like exacerbation of your daily symptoms, or difficulty navigating changing products due to inaccessibility.

Some of the ways you could make your periods slightly more comfortable or accessible could include:

- Work out which kind of period product is the most

sensory friendly for you. Some people find that period pants are more accessible as they are comfortable and easy to change, but others prefer disposable products they don't have to wash or touch after use.

- Using hot water bottles or heated lap pads.
- Try different types of movement if they are accessible to you, such as slow movement like yoga.
- Look after your sensory needs as you may find that other hypersensitivities or hyposensitivities are exacerbated during your period.

Eating and drinking

Eating and drinking is not always easy as a chronically ill and autistic person, for a huge variety of reasons – this can include needing to have a specific diet, certain habits or struggling with disordered eating. In this section we will look at some of these needs around eating and drinking and ideas about how to support yourself.

> I was diagnosed with colitis at 13, and discovered I was autistic when I was 44, so in between there have been a LOT of high-masked, safe-food cycles, along with some really disordered eating as I tried to stay healthy, AND be comfortable in a sensory way (without knowing that was what I was doing), AND be socially 'normal' with my eating (eating fries when people get fries for the table, or drinking when I was younger), AND live in a socially acceptable female body, all without full awareness of my own neurodivergence. – **Emily**

Habits around food
Many autistic people will find that they have certain 'safe foods' that they prefer to eat, whether that be because they are safe

in their taste or texture, or safe due to the familiarity that they provide.

Many autistic people will be seen by society as 'picky eaters', when most of our needs are not because we are trying to be fussy or difficult, but because our sensory needs are significant when it comes to food. For example, many may not like foods which don't have the same texture every time they eat them, or may not like a certain taste or texture like spiciness, creaminess or sourness.

There is nothing wrong with having safe foods or repeating the same meals. Whilst most allistic people might get bored of this or would think that you need variety, this is a very common habit for many autistic people, so it is not something you should feel ashamed of.

However, you may find that you need to think about making sure you are getting certain levels of nutrition and eating enough fibre, for example, particularly if you have a chronic illness that is impacted by what you eat.

It may be helpful for you to take vitamins or supplements to support your needs around nutrition if you are not able to eat foods which provide all of these different nutritional needs. This is something you may want to discuss with a doctor – some vitamins or supplements may need to be prescribed or monitored through blood tests, for example.

Sometimes, eating the same foods can be compatible with your chronic illness, like for Adam when dealing with his stoma:

> I basically eat the same things at the same times every day. Mostly because I know what the food is going to do, how it

will react with my stomach and stoma, and that it is unlikely
to cause blockages. This does create issues with my eating
disorder too though and it's a difficult balance... especially
if I am travelling as I cannot eat solid foods whilst travelling as it will either cause my stoma to work (too much) or
it will cause pain which will send me into sensory overload.
– **Adam**

Sensory needs vs. maintaining the needs of your chronic illness when eating or drinking

Many chronic illnesses come with ways of supporting symptoms
through food and drink. This can be much more difficult to deal
with when you are autistic and have sensory needs around this.
For example, you might need to:

- eat more salt
- eat more protein
- take in more electrolytes
- have NG/NJ (nasogastric/nasojejunal) tube or surgical
  tube feeding
- take medication that might be difficult to swallow.

As I take Metformin for PCOS, I should avoid simple carbohydrates as much as possible or risk adverse side effects
(exacerbated GI [gastrointestinal] issues). This clashes with
my autistic preference for bland same foods such as crisps,
potatoes and crackers. For the most part, I endure the GI
issues as I would rather do that than risk the sensory overload and discomfort that comes with trying to eat a more
balanced diet. This is a vicious cycle, however, because PCOS
increases the likelihood of weight gain, and its symptoms are
exacerbated by being overweight. This means my propensity

to use carbohydrates as same foods is more damaging as a person with PCOS, and it results in an exacerbation of PCOS symptoms (excess body hair, irregular periods, skin discolouration, headaches). – **Harriet**

Currently, my health needs include: maintaining a high enough calcium and protein intake to support my activity level and bone density, eating an adequate amount of calories to maintain a healthy weight, and avoiding foods that aggravate my gastroparesis and autoimmune gastrointestinal dysmotility (beef is the biggest offender) while consuming an adequate amount of fibre.

This may sound complicated, but one of the benefits of autism is that I am perfectly content eating the same foods every day. Once I optimised my diet to meet both my health needs and my taste preferences, I stuck to that. Importantly, my diet consists of easy-to-prepare foods, so I do not have to expend any cognitive resources choosing what to eat or preparing meals. This is a godsend when my cognitive dysfunction is acute. – **Dylan**

Some autistic people find unconventional methods of nutrition helpful to make sure they can support their needed diet, particularly if they are limited in the foods they can eat – for example, drinking smoothies, baby food pouches or clear protein, or using electrolyte tabs.

Some autistic people may need support to track their intake of something they need more of, as executive dysfunction can mean it is easy to forget what you have or haven't taken or eaten. Habit tracker apps may be helpful, or a physical reminder like a calendar or habit tracker stuck onto the fridge or cupboard where you keep them.

If you find medication difficult to swallow as tablets, you may find it helpful to ask if there is a liquid alternative, or find out if you can crush the medication into yoghurt, for example. Not every medication can be crushed, so make sure to ask your doctor before doing this.

JJ spoke to me about having an NJ tube due to having gastroparesis and how they manage it as an autistic person. They said:

> I have a nasojejunal (NJ) tube, which is a feeding tube that goes from my nose to my small intestine. I choose to have tubes placed by internal radiology, which involves using an x-ray machine to guide the tube into place, rather than by endoscopy, which involves a camera guiding the tube. I find the x-ray placement to be less anxiety-inducing and overwhelming as I am not sedated and can speak to the radiographers during the procedure.
>
> Having a feeding tube is an odd sensation. For the first week or so I could feel it constantly; it moved every time I spoke or drank water, and I relied heavily on throat sweets to soothe the scratchy feeling in my throat. I also found that swallowing would pull on the nose part of the tube, which was painful. Thankfully, the longer I've had the tube, the more my body has got used to it, and now I hardly notice it at all. When feeding or flushing the tube with water, I can feel the liquid moving through. It's cold on my cheek, and for the first few minutes of feeding I can feel it in my throat too.

I find distractions helpful, and I usually set my feeds to run overnight, so I'm asleep and it's more comfortable. I have patterned tapes that secure my tube to my face, and I enjoy matching my makeup or clothes to the tapes as it makes the tube feel less medical. I think the most uncomfortable aspect of having a tube is the public's reactions to it. I've had many strangers in public ask me about or make comments on the tube and why I have it; these can range from concern and curiosity, to anger and insults. I wish the public knew more about tube feeding and weren't so judgemental, and I wish medical professionals knew more about autism and took into account sensory needs, particularly during tube placement. – **JJ**

Becky also talked about how eating and drinking is impacted as an autistic person with Crohn's and POTS, both of which require some specific management with food and drink:

Due to my autism, I forget to drink as I sometimes do not get a thirst sensation which can cause issues for my POTS and heighten symptoms. My Crohn's can affect my eating as when in a flare I may have to eat special diets, such as liquid diets, plain diets and low FODMAP. This can become restrictive when layered on top of my eating preferences particularly around textures because of being autistic. My autism meant I could not manage the taste or texture of the liquid drinks needed for my Crohn's treatment, so I had to have a nasogastric feeding tube placed. – **Becky**

KEY TAKEAWAYS FROM THIS CHAPTER

- It is totally valid to have a combination of hypersensitivities and hyposensitivities, and to be sensory seeking and sensory averse, at the same time.
- There are not only five senses – there are also interoception, vestibular and proprioceptive senses which often need just as much support.
- There are lots of small accommodations you can put in place to try and support your sensory needs.
- Meltdowns, shutdowns and overstimulation are all exhausting. You may want to put plans in place for when these occur.
- Not all stims will be accessible to you, but there are ways to adapt them and still fulfil your sensory needs.
- Many autistic and chronically ill people can experience understimulation when resting. You might want to think about ways to combat this.
- Most of your experiences will be impacted by how your sensory needs interact with your chronic illnesses, including everything from periods to eating and drinking.

4

Pacing and routines

When I first started truly struggling with chronic fatigue, a few years after investigations into my pain and turned-in knees began, I was introduced to the idea of pacing – a way of looking at how we manage our energy levels over time.

Pacing is a technique commonly recommended to chronically ill people to try and prevent fatigue and pain or other symptoms from becoming overwhelming, potentially meaning you are less likely to 'crash' or be left in bed for days at a time. It might mean making adjustments to your work day by adding breaks, deciding to put activities in different orders, taking more rest time or not stacking lots of activities into one day. I can confirm that seven years on, I am certainly not perfect at it – but I have learnt a few things.

One of the reasons it has taken me so long to really grasp pacing as a concept has been because many aspects of traditional, professional-advised pacing do not account for the ways being autistic can impact it. Since that realisation, I've taken a lot of time to try and work out alternatives and see what works best for me.

> I don't consciously use pacing, or call it that, but I have a dry erase board in my house that has all the things for the

day on it, so I can see ahead of time what kind of day I'm about to have, and I'll make sure I take breaks accordingly. Like– if it's a day with four meetings in it, I'll have a very slow morning. Or if I have a doctor's appointment in the morning, and I'm teaching in the evening, then I'll plan to just read my book in between. – **Emily**

I experience post-exertional malaise, known as PEM. If I don't pace myself, my body WILL protest by crashing hard, so I suppose you could say pacing is effective – in the sense that if I don't do it, I can't continue and am forced to press pause for several days! I've found it inevitable that my physical and cognitive condition will crash and burn when I overdo it. It's hard not to overdo it because the amount of activity I can do doesn't remain consistent every day. There's always so much that needs doing, and my urge to Do Things when I have energy and am in less pain gets amplified by my guilt about being unable to do much most of the time, whether to contribute to the household or socialise with others. I still have a lot to work on in terms of learning to pace myself better, especially regarding listening to my body, and voicing and asserting my boundaries both to others and myself.

From many, many experiences, I have learnt that relentlessly pushing on my better days to make up for the worse ones will, without question, lead to another PEM crash, and many more worse days. It is much more sustainable – no, it is ONLY sustainable to pace myself. – **Dan**

Why is pacing recommended for chronically ill people?

The idea behind it is to prevent you from engaging in the 'boom and bust' model, which refers to when you use up all your energy in one day because you are having a good day with your symptoms. It can often feel like these days are few and far between as a chronically ill person, so it's no wonder that we want to get lots done, see friends or exercise on these days. However, because we perceive that we need to 'make the most' of the good day, we often overdo it, causing symptoms to then flare up in the days following.

Pacing, therefore, is a model that tries to prevent this. There are lots of different ways of tackling pacing and making it work for you, but it's general premise is to plan out your days in a way where you get enough rest, and making sure you don't push yourselves too far – whilst not being underactive either. Antcliff et al. advise that pacing is not only about how we plan activities and adjust them to our needs, but also how we accept the current limits of our abilities before looking at a gradual increase of them when our bodies are used to the activity.[1]

Your pacing should also not only be about work or education. You have to find what works for you through pacing or other theories or exercises so that you can live in a way that makes you as happy and comfortable as you can be. This could include things like hobbies or socialising, but it could also just be about self-care, eating or washing yourself. Some resources only discuss activities based on productivity or contribution to society, but your journey as a chronically ill autistic person should not be based on this – you are more than this, and your life deserves to be as well-rounded as you can make it alongside your needs.

Spoons and batteries

The 'spoon theory' of chronic illness was originated by Christine Miserandino in 2003.[2] During a dinner conversation when she was struggling to explain how her lupus impacted her, she picked up a set of spoons, and described the condition as having a limited set of 'spoons' compared to a healthy person. Each of these represents an amount of energy, with different tasks taking up a different amount. Brushing your hair might take one, but showering may take three – and you have to give up different activities depending on how many spoons you have left. Some days, you might have more than others.

For some people, the spoon theory works perfectly for them to describe their energy levels – it's quite logical, and some people like to physically work out how many spoons they are using in a day.

Personally, I have come to prefer a theory centred around batteries. For a healthy person, a good night's sleep will recharge their battery to 100 percent, just like a phone does when plugged in overnight. Perhaps if it's a bad night with more broken sleep, they might wake up at 90 percent instead.

Contrastingly, my battery will never get that high. I will always wake up with a maximum of, perhaps, 70 percent, and normally it's less than that. I never know what percentage I am going to wake up to.

If I use these theories, it is normally to explain my conditions to other people who have not encountered the ideas of chronic illnesses or chronic fatigue before, rather than as a way to decide how to structure my day. However, you might also find it a useful framework to start thinking about which activities are taking up your energy and how much you can normally do within a day.

How can I start pacing?

In order to start pacing, you first need to look at your current ability levels. You might find that if you have been stuck within the 'boom and bust' cycle for a while, you might have to try out activities in a different way to find out what your baseline of activity is before you cause a flare-up.

Baseline of activity refers to the amount of activity that you can do or cope with without it having an impact on your symptoms. For many, this can often be variable day to day, but you might have a certain set of activities, routines or an average day that you know your body can cope with when it is not in a flare-up.

You may find that certain activities can go hand-in-hand, whereas others need to be done on different days or hours apart. For example, you may not be able to cook on the same day that you do laundry, or you have to leave more time to rest if you have been for a doctor's appointment.

Think about your routines, and the things that are non-negotiable, for example any work or education you must attend. As autistic people, we are often more attached to our routines, so making sure these are accounted for can be very important – whether this be a morning routine, bedtime routine or something like a daily walk or time to stim that you want to build into the everyday.

Bigger activities should be broken down into smaller pieces, at least at the beginning, to understand what your limits are and consider whether you need to do everything at once. For example, you might think of 'hair and makeup' as one activity, when you could break it down into a lot more sections like base makeup and eyes with rest in between, if you needed to.

Sometimes, it's not as simple as just sitting down, timetabling out your day and sticking to it. In traditional pacing, you might give activities an energy rating and set out your day based on a limited amount of energy – but for many of us, our ability to do these activities might change every single day depending on a huge variety of factors. We will explore different forms of pacing later on in the chapter.

The main thing to remember is that pacing is different for every single person who tries it, because it depends on so many factors like the type of condition we have, which symptoms we are trying to reduce and how much energy you tend to have.

You should not expect to be good at pacing immediately, and you should be aware that you might be more tired at the start than usual because you are trying to put in more of a structure to your day that your body may not be used to. That's absolutely okay!

Lauren has started to try pacing with long Covid but is having to do so with no medical help. They said:

> I am starting to try using pacing to manage my fatigue levels, but haven't managed to access any medical help with my chronic illness so don't have any support with this. I have found that consistently doing less results in less crashes, instead of alternating between lots of activity and very little activity. – **Lauren**

Everyone will have different ways of pacing, or may not engage in pacing at all. It is something you can begin to do without a diagnosis or without input from others, if you feel it might be helpful.

MS told me about how they adapt pacing to work for them:

Pacing helps me to function in this world with the most minimum meltdowns and burnouts. For me, my daily life is far from routines. But I have some personal rules that I have to follow to be able to function in my max potential, if not, I would have severe burnouts after.

- For any activity – especially the major ones (going out of the house, working, groceries, meeting people, etc.), I have one max hour window to prepare and cool down (before and after the activity).
- I set my boundaries very strictly when it comes to plans. I try to stick on plans and schedules with discipline, not allowing sudden change of plans. In the case of emergency, I try to regulate myself to calm down (15 minutes to two hours, depends on how major the situation is) before interacting with others and making any decision.
- I have my strictly followed resting plans. During this time, I would try not to interact with anyone or do major tasks as much as I can, unless it's an emergency.
- In a professional situation, I strictly follow work hours and never compromise my health whenever I need to take a sick leave (and menstruation leave). – **MS**

How can autism impact pacing?

As someone with autism I struggle with change and the idea of using the pacing method felt like quite a substantial change and very daunting. I have however over time begun being able to use it and do use the method when going through periods of bad health. I have found the method effective, however I sometimes tailor it to fit my life and priorities. My advice for someone else trying to begin pacing is to write out the timings of your day and your priorities. You can then plan in what you want and need to do that day making sure you are well paced. Also ensuring you allow time to do things you would like to do! – **Becky**

There are several ways that being autistic can cause pacing to be a more difficult task.

You might struggle with executive dysfunction, which is when someone struggles with a range of things like planning, organisation, time management and getting started. This could mean that:

- you are more likely to be pushed into the boom-bust cycles previously discussed because you struggle with the planning element of pacing
- you may get distracted and do tasks for too long that you needed to do in shorter bursts
- you might find yourself sitting in front of a task unable to get started, using more of your precious energy on just desperately wanting to do something than actually doing it. This can be compounded with brain fog too.

Similarly, you may find that if you're an autistic person who likes routines, pacing may not fit well with these processes, because you have to move things or leave them out to rest instead. Your desire to continue your routines might mean you over-exert yourself when you might need rest.

There are also sensory needs that can impact pacing, too. Firstly, if you begin to experience sensory overload or overwhelm during your task, you may be interrupted and not be able to finish it, causing you to need to do things during rest blocks or simply meaning you are even more tired than normal. You might also be someone who hates resting because you feel understimulated.

Another sensory need could be if you are someone who struggles with interoception, which is a topic we covered in Chapter 1. You might not realise when your body is beginning to become too tired or painful until it is too late, so you might push through more of your activity than you should.

> I don't really have the executive functioning ability to build in any pacing system beyond taking breaks in the moment. I struggle to stick with schedules and plan, so I just try my best to listen to my body. It isn't easy though. I'm notoriously bad at looking after myself and resting. I tend to keep going until I crash and get ill or burn out.
>
> I've been doing my best to improve on this though by thinking more about the tasks that I find tiring and trying to make sure that I don't do too many of them in one day. Asking for support from the people around me has been essential. They often have a better awareness of when I need to pace myself than I do. – **Eli**

Methods of pacing that might help

There are a few different ways you could mitigate these issues.

One is a form of pacing called *energy switching*, which might help with the understimulation that comes with rest, as well as possibly helping some of the executive dysfunction. This is when instead of doing an activity and then a block of complete rest doing nothing, you switch between tasks which take up different kinds of energy. For example, you might read a book after putting on a load of laundry, and then do something that is more akin to rest, like listening to a podcast or music, or listening to a guided meditation.

You might also find it helpful to write out your to-do list and look at how much energy each task might take you – some people might do this with a *traffic light* or *numbering system*. You can then work out how many of these tasks you will be able to stack during a day. For example, you might be able to do one high-energy task and one low-energy task, or three medium ones, depending on how you are feeling that day.

Some might also use *time limits*, which can help if you struggle with your interoception and feel like you won't be able to work out when to naturally stop. You could use the Pomodoro Technique for this. This is traditionally set out as being where you work for 20 minutes and then have a 5 minute break, with a longer 15 minute break after four sessions, but you might find that you need shorter work sessions and longer breaks instead, and just use the general structure as a pacing support.

Boom and bust cycles

Even those who have pacing down to a T will occasionally fall into a boom and bust period. We all have times that are busier, or meetings that come out of nowhere, or deadlines that suddenly fall into our laps that didn't exist when you planned out your week. This isn't something to be ashamed of, and it doesn't mean you are failing to cope with the nature of your conditions.

However, what you might be able to do is avoid your life being a continual boom and bust cycle, where you cannot seem to even out your activity and are constantly flaring up or crashing, which can be very difficult to cope with.

Part of avoiding this can be in not over-packing your calendar with events. But you may not be falling into these cycles because of this – you may simply be doing too much when you perceive you are having a 'good day' and want to do more.

It might feel much easier to fall into these patterns as an autistic person for a variety of reasons – due to your interoception and not processing the warning signals of your body, or because you want to complete your tasks and routines.

What about special interests?

'Special interests' in autistic people tend to refer to a very intense and highly focused interest, but 'interest' here does not only refer to topics, it can also be an activity. For example, mine are in *Six the Musical*, watching elite world gymnastics, and Alice Oseman, but I know people who have them in crocheting or embroidery. These tend not only to be something we spend a lot of time on or are very invested in, but they also are a huge part of how we regulate ourselves. We often use these to bring calmness or order to ourselves when things feel stressful or overwhelming, or when emotions are heightened.

When it comes to pacing, special interests are definitely some-thing you should make time for – they can have a huge impact on how you feel about the rest of life, and as a chronically ill per-son they might help you to accept your condition or distract you from difficult symptoms.

Something many autistic people find can happen is that when they are doing something to do with their special interests, they will get sucked in and become hyperfocused, so they end up working on it for hours. 'Hyperfocus' refers to intense concentration that completely focuses on a task or topic, and it can be very difficult to pull away from this. If someone interrupts you during this period it can make you jolt or feel very disconcerted.

Having special interests is a great part of being autistic because it can be incredibly liberating and beautiful to be so invested and knowledgeable about a topic you love, but when you are also chronically ill it can be difficult to navigate the way that this hyperfocus might make you overtired, fatigued or cause pain.

You might find therefore that you have to have ways to mitigate this. You could use time limits and alarms, or you could make sure you are in a comfortable position and environment before you start.

Flare-up or autistic burnout?

Sometimes the combination of being chronically ill and autistic can lead to situations that look very similar but come from different roots. Sometimes, this doesn't matter too much because ultimately it's all in your one, same body – but sometimes, you might need to put different supports in place depending on what is happening.

One situation of this can be a flare-up of chronic symptoms compared to autistic burnout.

Autistic burnout is a feeling of absolute exhaustion, whether physical, mental or emotional. A lot of autistic people say that it tends to come from the impact of navigating a neurotypical world.

Autistic burnout is different to the burnout allistic people often discuss (which we can also experience) because it can include:

- Loss of skills including social or daily living skills

- Making you more prone to sensory overload more quickly
- Physical, emotional and mental exhaustion
- An increase in emotional dysregulation, anxiety or suicidality
- Feeling unable to speak

Often this cannot go away simply with physical rest alone.

Unlike burnout that is a result of working too hard, autistic burnout tends to be a product of consistent sensory overstimulation, masking or executive functioning difficulties.

Autistic burnout can last for long periods of time, sometimes even years.

You might find that being in a state of autistic burnout can cause chronic flare-ups to become more regular or more difficult as you are already in a state of sensory or emotional exhaustion that runs your body down. Similarly, having flare-ups can make you more susceptible to autistic burnout.

When either one of these is starting they can feel very similar for me – my fatigue increases and my tolerance for sensory input decreases, amongst other things. I tend to put supports in place for both if I am unsure which it will be, especially because they can end up in a cycle regardless.

Some of the ways you can pre-emptively put in supports include:

- Reducing activity including social and physical (this is not just about going out or seeing friends, it can also be reduction of physical activity like simplifying skincare routines or leaving out less time-crucial activities like vacuuming)

- Using my accommodations more at work and university, such as extensions or watching my lectures online
- Spending more time on sensory regulation and sensory seeking
- Engaging with your special interests
- Eating safe foods and finding ways of making cooking and eating easier (see Chapter 3 for more on this)
- Leaning more on support networks (this can be in many different ways, whether this is practical support or simply checking in via messages)
- Making sure to take medication and supplements as prescribed and needed, and gently doing my physio
- Using communication supports of Augmentative and Alternative Communication

This is arguably one of the places where chronic illness and autism intertwine the most and become the most confusing to work out what to do. Some might find they are able to differentiate this with time whilst others may find this more difficult.

Stimming and pacing

We already covered what stimming is in Chapter 3, but it is important to mention it in the context of pacing too.

I would recommend that stimming is noted as a part of your pacing, particularly if it is an activity that will take more energy, such as spinning or using a trampoline. It may only take a small amount of your energy, but that is still something you need to be aware of.

If you are using the energy switching method of pacing, you might find that stimming takes a role as one of the forms of energy you are using.

What might a standard day look like?

I like to follow the energy switching mode of pacing. My day might look like any combination of these activities:

- One hour: emails and admin
- Two to three hours: meetings (normally Teams or Zoom as I work from home)
- One to two hours: laptop work and writing
- One hour of reading or colouring in the middle of the day to rest without boredom
- One to two hours of watching TV or YouTube
- Making sure to add in some time for stimming of some sort, whether that be with fidget toys, a short walk or dancing around my room

I find that I often work in the morning, then take the afternoon to rest and recharge, and then find that I might be able to do some more work later on in the day and into the evening. This is just because of how my energy patterns tend to look, so this is something you should consider and try to learn as you go along. It took me quite a few years of crashing out in the afternoon to learn that I probably shouldn't force myself to work at that time.

We will discuss work boundaries in more detail in Chapter 5, but you may find that some of your pacing depends on your ability to implement your own boundaries within your job or education. For example, I am privileged enough to mostly choose my own hours, which many people will not get to do.

You might not have a standard day, whether that be because you have a job or university timetable that is all over the place, or because you just don't like your days to be the same. You also might have children or caring responsibilities that change your day-to-day life and limit how much you can do this. That's perfectly valid too! You might find it more helpful to time block in a calendar, putting in blocks for each activity when it is convenient or preferred, but also making sure to block in that rest time.

You might have some days that are heavier than others. For example, I volunteer on a Friday evening, so I tend to do less during the day in order to make sure I have the energy to go out later on. If you were to be working a night shift, for example, the next day may be much more rest-heavy to compensate.

Know that shortcuts are okay

You may find that sometimes you physically cannot do it all – and that's okay. If you had a university deadline, you might have to leave your email inbox for a day or two, or maybe you wouldn't do any laundry for those few days.

If your version of pacing means that you eat a ready meal or takeaway rather than cooking, that is okay. So is using dry shampoo instead of showering if you need to prioritise work one day and you know that showering is a task that takes a lot of your energy.

The point of pacing, to me at least, is not to find a way for you to suddenly manage to do everything. Pacing is not a sudden fix to your issues of not having enough energy to do things. It is absolutely okay for you to take shortcuts that make your day easier.

Some other shortcuts, life hacks or supports that might help you could include:

- Having phone chargers and water bottles in different rooms so you don't have to find them
- Having snacks available easily
- Buying pre-chopped or frozen vegetables
- Doing your work in bed

- Using wet wipes
- Listening to audiobooks or having a light e-reader instead of reading heavy physical copies
- Having a bag ready with what you need to leave the house

Working in bed and the lies of capitalism

You might see that I listed 'do your work in bed' as a shortcut or support as a chronically ill autistic person and have thought that that's something you cannot or should not do. Now, this will not be for everyone. For some people, they may find that their sleep becomes poorer due to the association of work with the bed space. However, for many of us, we sometimes just need to work in bed because we physically cannot work sitting at a desk at that time.

Capitalism tells us we couldn't possibly be productive working from bed, because we will want to nap or we will become sleepy. This isn't necessarily true, and for those of us struggling with chronic fatigue and pain when at an uncomfortable desk, the option of working in bed means that we can at least do *some* work, where not doing so might mean we cannot do anything.

Of course, this is not always the best thing to do. If you are fatigued or in pain and need to be in bed for a proper rest, you should not be pushing yourself to work. Long term, working all the time is not sustainable and is not what you should be doing. This advice is more for you when you are wanting to work and are trying to manage working, not as a substitute for resting. Sometimes a proper break is needed, and that is important too.

Coping when your routine is changed by chronic illness

Many autistic people find it comforting to have a set structure and routine, as it means their life is more predictable and within their control. However, when you also have a chronic illness, you might find that this is less easy to uphold due to interruptions, such as:

- Symptoms, like pain, fatigue or dislocations – and tasks taking longer because of them
- Needing more rest than usual
- Having a flare-up which interrupts you for longer periods of time
- Doctor's appointments, tests or therapies

One way you might be able to navigate this is by not having a set routine or timetable for the whole day, and instead having shorter routines which you can do at any time. For example, you might have a 'morning' routine for getting out of bed, getting washed and dressed, and having breakfast. This could be a set of actions that form a routine, but isn't always done at the same time of day.

You might find it useful to have specific routines for doctor's appointments or therapies. I have a pre-physio routine of changing my clothes, doing my hair, filling my water bottle and making sure I have my sunflower lanyard and keys. Having this as a determined set of actions means I am able to transition into the emotional and physical space for physio, even though it isn't always at the same time of the day every week.

If tasks are sometimes taking you longer than when you are at your baseline, it may help to block more time for them as standard – if you finish things more quickly, then you have that time back, and this is hopefully less stressful than if something takes longer than planned.

Having to take multiple days of rest during a flare-up or crash can be frustrating for anyone, but for autistic people, being away from our routines or standard days can feel difficult or even painful. To help with this, you could have a routine that you implement during flare-ups, which might include changing into fresh pyjamas, using wet wipes and applying deodorant alongside something that makes you happy without using as much energy, like listening to an audiobook.

Emotional regulation can also be significantly difficult as an autistic and chronically ill person, and routine changes can make this more prominent. You might find yourself feeling dysregulated, depressed or anxious when there are changes.

Different people find different supports for this, which might include meditation or breathwork, stimming, finding activities to distract yourself like colouring in, watching a comfort show or using tools like a weighted blanket. On a more long-term level, therapy or learning coping skills can also help. I recommend the *Neurodivergent Friendly Workbook of DBT Skills* by Sonny Jane Wise (2022).

KEY TAKEAWAYS FROM THIS CHAPTER

- Pacing is not one size fits all – it's likely you will have to do a lot of trial and error before you get it right.
- It is okay if pacing is harder for you as an autistic person – work alongside your traits like special interests and stimming.
- Sometimes working in bed is okay, and isn't something to be ashamed of or avoid just because society says it isn't effective.
- You might need different routines for different situations.
- You are allowed to use shortcuts – it doesn't make you lazy.
- Navigating a neurotypical/allistic society is exhausting and it's valid to acknowledge that.

Pacing example for someone who works from home and uses energy switching

9am: Morning routine and breakfast (★ ★)

10am:

    Zoom calls for work with short breaks (★ ★ ★)

11am:

12pm: Listen to audiobook and eat easy lunch (★)

1pm: Sensory regulation and physical rest (★)

2pm:

    Work tasks using Pomodoro Technique (★ ★ ★)

3pm:

4pm: Wrap up tasks for the day (★ ★)

5pm: Watch TV or read a book (★ / ★ ★)

6pm: Make and eat dinner (★ ★)

7pm: Spend time with family (★ / ★ ★)

8pm: Wind down and night routine (★)

Pacing example for someone who has to work in shift patterns, pacing around this as possible

9am: Morning routine and breakfast

10am: ⎡

11am: | Work shift

12pm: ⎣

1pm: Lunch break – rest and sensory regulation

2pm: ⎡

        Work shift

3pm: ⎣

4pm: Travel home and decompress

5pm: ⎡

        Rest as needed – sensory, physical or other
        (e.g. read book or listen to music)

6pm: ⎣

7pm: Make and eat dinner

8pm: Wind down and night routine

5

Education and employment

Flexible schedules, working from home, and leveraging your strengths to overcome your challenges is the advice you often see, but for how many people is this realistic? We need systemic change. We need to make it easier for people to request and receive the accommodations they need. We need to make applying for disability [support or benefits] less difficult and demoralising. – **Dylan**

Many autistic and chronically ill people will struggle with institutions like schooling and being employed. These spaces generally have ableism baked into their structures, affecting us at an institutional level. It is not always the case that we can access them at all – which is a failure of society and its systems, not of ourselves.

However, there are some ways in which we can adjust how we interact with these places and find ways to make them more accessible to us, which we will discuss throughout this chapter.

As a current university student, I have struggled over the years to work out how I can make the environment I'm in work for me, instead of me trying to work with it in ways that made me more unwell or pushed me into autistic burnout. I also work in a freelance manner, which can be more accessible for some.

Different options for work and school will be explored here, as what is right for you may be very different to another chronically ill autistic – even if they have the same conditions.

Navigating the education system

> Once I was diagnosed with Crohn's disease I began missing weeks to months of school at a time, and my autism meant I found it hard to deal with the uncertainty linked to my Crohn's and treatments. This led to me struggling to attend school even more. I also have struggled with sitting exams due to being too unwell to attend school. I was allowed to do some of my exams at home however and had alternative arrangements for any I undertook at school. – **Becky**

Because education systems up to the age of 16 are often very rigid and structured, there are both positives and negatives for chronically ill and autistic individuals who are trying to survive them. Many of us thrive off having routines in place for us in an environment that is predictable, but many aspects of these systems can be inaccessible or push us into sensory overload or cause chronic symptoms to flare under pressure.

The sensory environment
We discussed sensory needs in detail in Chapter 3, but there are some aspects in particular that can pop up in education settings. This might include:

- Struggling with noises like shouting or alarms/bells
- Having issues with practical lessons like music, art or physical education
- Struggling to navigate around buildings, getting lost or feeling trapped

- Hating scratchy clothing and finding it distracting
- Getting easily overwhelmed or struggling to focus
- Struggling with bright lights

There are many accommodations and aids that can be put in place to support sensory needs and difficulties in the school environment. It should be made clear that these will be different for every single student, and sometimes it can take time to find what works.

Teachers of chronically ill and autistic students should try to be understanding of these ever-changing needs and help put accommodations in place as necessary. They should try to remember that a student acting in a different way to a non-disabled or allistic student does not mean they are automatically not engaged or not focusing.

They should also be aware of the fact that every student is different and has varying needs and wants for these accommodations – they shouldn't be put in place without some discussion and understanding of whether or not they will be helpful.

Here are just a few ways that the sensory needs of chronically ill and autistic students could be supported:

- Allow the student to leave a class slightly early, so they can navigate the halls before they become loud and full of people.
- Allow the student to take time out of a class if they become overwhelmed or if they need to take medication.
- Allow the student to go to the toilet as needed.
- Have a space or spaces available that a student can go to in these cases that is quiet, safe and calm. They may need these for short periods to regulate, or they may sometimes need these as places to do their work.
- Give the student extra time to navigate tasks in practical lessons, or excuse them from them if more appropriate.

- Allow the student to wear alternative clothing.
- Allow the student to doodle or use fidget toys in class.
- Talk to the student about where is best for them to sit in the classroom. Some may prefer to be at the back so they can see the whole environment, whereas others may want to be at the front.
- Try different aids out, such as pencil grips if they struggle with proprioception, or coloured paper or overlays if they struggle visually. It may help to use worksheets which have less visual clutter on them; some may struggle to process PowerPoints on the computer and may need them printed.
- Allow use of earplugs or ear defenders.

Pastoral care

Dealing with education is, of course, not just about the education itself, nor the classroom. Navigating education means navigating being around your peers, trying to make friends and dealing with breaktimes, for example.

Teachers should support autistic and chronically ill students in a pastoral manner in ways such as:

- Discussing a student's needs *with* them and not deciding what they are *for* them
- Providing additional information or support with anything happening outside of the normal day, like trips, exams or assemblies
- Dealing with bullying effectively and supporting young people with friendships and loneliness
- Treating information confidentially and not discussing needs in front of other students
- Providing safe spaces for students to talk to you and making sure they are aware these are available

Many autistic and chronically ill students may not find it easy to seek out help or come up to teachers to talk. It can be helpful to have someone who checks in regularly and provides that space before asking, so that issues can be sorted out earlier.

Scheduling and the school day

Being a chronically ill and autistic student can mean it often feels like there are constant barriers and blocks to getting through a school day. For me, I will find myself constantly worrying about the next thing happening, unable to focus on the current as there is so much to process and consider.

There are a few ways teachers and students can work together to make the school day more manageable and easier to process:

- Have a clear timetable which details the times, rooms and any equipment needed.
- Let the student know as soon as possible if there are any changes to any of the above.
- Homework and coursework should have clear deadlines to avoid confusion, but extensions should be easily discussed if needed due to chronic symptoms or overwhelm.
- Visual schedules or social stories can help some autistic people to process schedules better.
- If possible, rooms should be close together to avoid the student having to walk very far between sessions, which could cause sensory overload and exacerbate chronic symptoms.
- Have somewhere the student can put extra equipment so they don't have to carry it around for the whole day which could cause additional pain or fatigue.
- Consider where would be best for the student to be during breaks or lunchtimes. Dining rooms or playgrounds can cause sensory overwhelm and mean the student cannot access the rest of their classes.
- If needed, consider part-time or reduced schedules. It

may be that if there are free periods or inaccessible lessons that these are taken off the student's timetable and used for resting or going home early.

Alice is a sixth form student who is studying for A Levels (British qualifications studied after age 16). She talked about her experience of schooling:

> There's the societal expectation you will always be doing something. In sixth form I've had frees, so I can go to the common room and crash if I need to but there's an expectation for you to be constantly working. I want to do all my hobbies outside of school, I don't want to lose myself and my personality to doing my A Levels. At the weekends, I can sleep for 13 hours and it doesn't matter.
>
> I schedule in rest into my calendar but there's a lack of understanding by non-disabled people about pacing. They don't realise I have to go home and go to sleep because I'm so tired.
>
> The system is not built for you to be disabled, or be autistic. If you don't fit in the box then you really struggle. Systemic issues are ignored and are still evident in the education system. – **Alice**

Practical lessons

There are a variety of practical lessons done in schooling that may be difficult for chronically ill and autistic students – for example, physical education, cookery, textiles, woodworking, art and music.

It should be noted that although there are adjustments that can be made for these lessons, in some cases, these may not be enough and the lesson will be inaccessible. Teachers should be willing to understand this and make alternative arrangements.

Some of the ways chronically ill and autistic young people could be supported to engage in practical lessons include:

- Being given extra support from a teacher, or extra time as needed
- Understanding that some elements may be more difficult than others to engage in – sometimes you may need to remove part of the task but not the whole task
- Being given instructions in alternative manners – in smaller, more manageable chunks or in visual ways, for example
- Finding alternative ways for them to be involved – such as refereeing or umpiring instead of partaking in sports
- Being supported to lift heavy objects or deal with tasks which take coordination, such as moving trays out of an oven
- Using adapted equipment, like pencil grips or adapted cooking equipment

Revision and studying

Much like non-disabled students revise in different ways depending on what works for them, many autistic and chronically ill students will all find different things that help them to study. What might be significantly different to your non-disabled peers, however, is the adaptations you have to make in order for studying to be accessible, effective and sustainable.

In Chapter 4, we discussed pacing techniques and ways to conserve and work with your energy levels. Some of these may apply to your study methods; for example, you may want to use the Pomodoro Technique or an adapted method of it to make sure that you do not spend too long studying in one go and include breaks. You might also find that you need to study in bed, or not sit up for long periods whilst studying.

Some other ideas that you could experiment with to try and make studying more accessible include:

- Using online programmes instead of handwriting, such as typing up your notes, using flashcard programmes or using mindmap software
- Using speech to text software, where you speak instead of typing out yourself
- Using software that reads text out to you to lessen processing
- Using muted or pastel colours to lessen visual intake, and similarly trying out overlays or coloured paper to see if this may also help your processing needs
- Trying a variety of study methods to see which works best for you, as well as understanding which take more energy to help you know which you could do on days where you don't feel as well
  - For example, reading, watching YouTube videos, listening to podcasts or doing short question and answer flashcards may be more accessible on bad days than longer tasks like doing past exam questions
- Placing flashcards or posters around your bedroom or around your house so you can read over them often

If you are given study leave before exam periods, this may be a help, a hindrance or a combination of both depending on your needs. For some, this gives an opportunity to rest more around your exams and go at your own pace. However, some may find that they struggle to focus or provide their own structure in these times. You may want to speak to your school and see if you can be given more support with this.

Exams and assessments

Exams and assessments can be difficult for a variety of reasons as an autistic and chronically ill student, often because they are very long and require a lot of writing – both of these factors can exacerbate lots of symptoms of chronic illnesses – as well as the environment often causing sensory overwhelm, anxiety and executive functioning differences.

There are many ways that exams and assessments can be adapted. Many education systems and exam boards require that these be formally applied for and assessed, so unfortunately not all of them will be accessible to everyone. However, some ways to make these situations work better for you that can sometimes be approved might include:

- Having extra time, or rest breaks throughout testing
- Being in a separate room, so you can move around and be exposed to less sensory input; alternatively, being sat where you are most comfortable such as away from doors or at the back or front of a room
- Using a word processor instead of writing, or having a scribe to write for you
- Having someone who reads questions out to you
- Having adaptive or supportive equipment, such as a writing slope or pen grips
- Having access to regulated memory materials
- Using stim toys, ear defenders or sensory equipment like weighted lap pads or vests
- For exams with a listening portion, such as for languages, it may be helpful to use headphones rather than listening to a speaker due to sensory needs
- If you have a condition where management includes needing to eat or drink, this should be allowed

As well as this, there are some ways you might be able to make exams better for yourself which do not require regulation, such as:

- Wearing multiple layers, so you can remove or add them if temperature regulation is difficult or you don't know what the room temperature will be like
- Having a checklist or visual timetable for before and after the test, so you know you have everything you need and know what the structure of the day is
- Using a highlighter or underlining words or phrases to help you focus on questions, and having extra paper to help you plan, process and understand what you are doing
- Having a watch with you to visually process time passing (or being in front of a clock in the room)
- Visiting the rooms your exam will take place in before the exam period so you know what it will look like and how it will feel
- Making sure you rest more before your exam, and decompress afterwards
- Reading the whole paper before beginning the exam can sometimes help as you are more aware of what is coming up next

University and moving away from home

If you go to university, some of the previous sections in this chapter will apply to university education, as they will to school or college. However, university tends to change more about your life than just being educated in a different venue. Many who go to university will move away from living at home and be living on their own, which can add responsibilities and often different pressures on your life as a chronically ill and autistic individual.

University isn't the right environment for everyone, both because of the system itself not being as supportive as it should be or simply because it may not be the type of learning you want to do. It is totally valid to go down other routes even though society pushes us towards higher education.

> I dropped out of uni. This was prior to becoming chronically ill in the way I am now, though it contributed to it a lot. Undiagnosed ADHD was rendering me unable to study or complete assignments. The complete change of environment – a different town away from my support system and everyone I knew, living with a bunch of strangers and away from my family, a drastically different educational structure that was less consistent than the Monday to Friday 8:30am–3:30pm of secondary school, having to cook every meal myself, having to look after the house because my new flatmates neglected it – completely burnt me out, on top of the burnout I already had from A Levels. – **Dan**

Choosing a university

Every university will have different pros and cons – and that goes for everyone, not just disabled students. The quality of the education, whether they do subjects you want to do, the accommodation and the nightlife are all things that everyone has to weigh up when choosing their university, but being disabled adds a whole host of other factors. You might need to consider:

- The physical accessibility of the environment
- The academic support for disabled students
- Whether there is accommodation that is or can be made right for your needs
- If there is a community of disabled students
- Healthcare (if you are moving to a new place and need continued care)
- Transport around the city
- Proximity of things you need to each other (e.g. the university, supermarket, doctors, library)

Some disabled people find that a university that is campus-based rather than across a city can be helpful as there is less need for travelling around and means everything is more accessible and you need less time to get where you need to be. A campus is also often a flatter terrain, or if it is not, it is more built up and will be more physically accessible, with ramps and lifts, for example.

Most universities will have lots of information available online, but there are other ways you can gain additional information. For instance, there are hundreds of people who document their experiences on social media, YouTube or on forums, which will give you real-life insight into what it is like to attend there. In terms of your disabilities, it can be helpful to get in contact with the disability service itself as they are expert on how their particular school will be able to help you.

If you can, it can be extremely helpful to physically visit the university and the city it is in. This might not be possible for everyone, or it may not be possible to see every place you are considering applying to, but it can help you to understand the accessibility better as you can navigate it in person and see how the buildings and accommodation look or work – pictures don't always tell the full story!

Lauren told me about being autistic and having long Covid at university, studying a subject that is impacted by their symptoms. They said:

I have to study mostly remotely, maybe only being on campus one day a week, and I use a tablet to highlight lecture slides and course notes instead of making my own notes. For my exams, I have my own room with my disability advisor as my invigilator, and have 25 percent extra time and 10 minute rest breaks per hour of exam. I also have extra exam materials such as course notes, and an altered exam paper so that there is less focus on memorisation. My education is impacted a lot, especially because I study physics which is very memory-reliant. In fact, it used to be a special interest, but now due to chronic illness, I will not be able to go into physics anymore. – **Lauren**

Picking a course for university is not always simple for autistic and chronically ill people. You might have passions or interests you want to follow, but feel like you won't be able to keep up due to your memory, your fatigue or your sensory needs, for example. I chose a university where my course has more coursework than exams due to my memory and struggling to work under timed conditions, which I have found helpful. You can also consider whether a remote course is more helpful, and if courses with practicals can be made accessible to you, as we will explore in the rest of the chapter.

I studied my degree full-time for two years, then took a year out, and am now studying the last two years part-time. There are lots of different ways to do a degree that aren't just three years full-time.

Before you move to university

There are lots of ways you can try and make sure you are as prepared as possible for university, from the application process to what you take with you. Here is a checklist for ways you can prepare for university:

☐ Inform your university of your disability and how it impacts you. Most will have a process in which to define a plan to support you to engage with your studies.
☐ Check for any grants or scholarships you may be entitled to as a disabled student. For example, in the UK, Disabled Students' Allowance.

☐ Consider whether you have any care needs that need to move with you. This might be having carers or moving the centre of your medical care.

☐ Do an audit for a few days at home being aware of your needs and note everything you might need help with or need an aid or accommodation for. Make sure you have all of these supports ready to go.
  - You may need to experiment with trying different aids, particularly for tasks you have not had to do alone before. We will explore these further in the 'living independently' section of this chapter.

☐ You may want to visit the university and get used to the surroundings and, if possible, visit your accommodation so you feel more comfortable and settled when you arrive.

Your first weeks at university

Everyone tends to talk about the first weeks of university as the best weeks of their experience, but even for non-disabled students this is often not really the case. These weeks are often emotional and very busy, and there is a lot of change to get used to all at once. This can be particularly different for us as chronically ill and autistic students who struggle with new environments, new social situations and learning to balance our chronic symptoms with wanting to still get involved in university life.

The first few weeks being so busy can also mean you struggle with managing your needs, such as making sure you eat. It can be helpful to prepare for this by having easy options available that you can microwave or cook quickly. Similarly, you may be more likely to forget medications or treatments. It might help to have these prepared in advance and set out somewhere you can see easily, or have a checklist, to help you not lose your grip on these.

It can be difficult to know when to keep going and be involved in everything and when to rest. It is important to find this balance because you may miss out on small things happening, but if you don't look after yourself, you are more likely to experience flare-ups or burnout that mean you have to stop engaging completely for much longer periods of time.

You might want to consider whether you tell new people you meet about your disabilities. For those who are visibly disabled or use mobility aids, there is less of a choice as to whether anyone will notice, but you may still prefer not to give details. Sometimes it can feel safer not to tell people about being autistic or disabled, and sometimes it may be that you feel a sense of security with the knowledge that someone knows if something were to go wrong. You may want to tell those you are living with but not those in your classes, for example.

The first few weeks of university also tend to include lots of students drinking alcohol. For many of us who are autistic and chronically ill, alcohol can cause issues – it may make us dizzy or exacerbate our symptoms, heighten our sensory needs, make us anxious or react with our medications, as a few examples. You can engage with events without drinking alcohol – although the culture around it may feel pressuring, most will accept you saying no and many universities will put on separate events for those who do not want to drink or engage in nightlife, for example doing game, film or craft nights. If the university is not putting anything like this on, you may find that there are groups of you from your accommodation who will get together and do things like this instead.

If you do engage in nightlife, such as going to bars or clubbing, you might want to find ways to make this more accessible. For example:

- Wearing earplugs or ear defenders
- Staying hydrated throughout
- Going for rest breaks or fresh air periodically
- Going home earlier than others might

- Having your medications and any bedtime routines set out for you
- Wearing a sunflower lanyard, having a Medical ID on your phone, or having cards on you which detail your conditions in case there are any problems during the events

Dealing with lack of structure and changes to routine at university

Many university students can find themselves struggling with having less structure given to them than they had in school, especially given the amount of new errands and responsibilities they may now have to fit in. This is particularly true for autistic people, who may prefer life to have a lot of structure and routine, and chronically ill people who might need to self-manage their conditions to a specific structure (whether that be taking medications at a specific time, or having symptoms that are exacerbated by issues like changes to sleep, as examples).

You might find that you have to experiment with your routine in the first few weeks, which can unfortunately mean feeling more disorientated than usual for a while.

Here are a few ways to try and reduce this:

- Have strong morning and evening routines. If the middle of your day is chaotic and changing, this can help anchor you to the rest of the day.
- Use checklists or visual timetables to visualise and understand your days.
- Find a planner or calendar that works for you. You might like to put plans on pen and paper, have them digitally or a mix of both; you also may need to work out the format.
- Start to build your routines around your timetabled lessons and any other set sessions such as society meetings or therapy appointments.

Some university students like to treat university like a job, doing university work between set hours. For some, this might be a 9–5 structure, but for many autistic and chronically ill people this might be too ambitious. You might like to do mornings or afternoons, or prefer to do a few hours, have a break and then do a few more in the evening. It doesn't matter what it looks like – it just may help to have set hours dedicated to university.

Others will do something different every day depending on how many classes they have, or around errands or jobs they need to do once a week or once every fortnight. For example, you might need to do laundry once a week, or make time for a food shop every two.

Due to autistic and chronically ill people commonly struggling with sleep, whether due to fatigue, insomnia, painsomnia or running treatments throughout the night, it can be helpful for some to try and wake up at the same time each day and wind down at the same time at night regardless of whether you have classes. This is because for some people sleeping in later or winding down later can have a longer-term impact on sleep patterns and impact symptoms. This might not be practical every single day, but it might be something to consider within your new structures.

Many chronically ill students will have physiotherapy or exercise programmes they have to put in place themselves. This can be difficult due to the motivation and executive function it takes to do it, as well as it causing a knock-on effect on your symptoms afterwards. You might need to consider where this is placed in your routine for these reasons – it might need to be at the end of your day of classes, or on less heavy days, for example.

Amber told me about her experience of university and trying to deal with lack of structure and getting support:

Several elements of the academic side of university can be quite tricky at times; most of my struggles stem from the self-directed nature of it. I need specific instructions of what to do/what is expected of me as lots of choice and vague instructions can get me into a bit of a pickle. For example, often we will be given lots of options for reading tasks and will only be expected to do a couple of them, but without specific instruction about which ones are the most useful/important I can struggle to prioritise because my brain decides it wouldn't be an option if it wasn't important and then I try and read them all – which nine times out of ten comes at a detriment to managing my chronic illness symptoms.

I have been fortunate that staff at my university, both disability services and academic, have been really supportive of providing reasonable adjustments for both my chronic illnesses and autism. All teaching staff receive a comprehensive document outlining all the ways they can best support me in their classroom, which was put together by disability services with my input. This has helped me hugely in managing my workload, communicating my needs and my ability to engage in taught sessions more comfortably.

In seeking support, I think my biggest advice would be keeping in the front of your mind that you are entitled to support – you are not being difficult by asking for your access needs to be met! Beyond that, communicate what you need in the way that is easiest for you – you might find it easier to verbalise this in an in-person meeting, via email or in a written list. Also, you don't have to do this independently, you could ask a trusted person to help you coordinate asking for support, they might even have some suggestions of things you could ask about if they know you and what helps you manage your conditions well. – **Amber**

Living independently

Not every autistic and chronically ill individual can live alone, and it is completely valid if you can't – it doesn't make you a failure or make you childish, it simply means that you have access needs that have to be met which you can't make work living alone.

If you are able to or wanting to live alone, university may be a good first taste of this. For some, it can be the best environment for you to try to do so, because there are often heightened security and welfare measures to look after you – more than you would have living in a standard flat.

There are also other ways of moving out safely and independently – like moving close to your family, moving in with friends or having the support of carers.

Living independently can bring along a wealth of responsibilities that you may not have had previously, including (but not limited to): doing laundry, cooking, managing medical appointments, paying rent or bills, doing food shopping or changing bedding.

Some of these things may come more easily to you than others do, for a variety of reasons – whether due to struggling to physically navigate something, struggling with executive dysfunction or being someone who struggles to talk on the phone, as just a few examples.

Some autistic and chronically ill people may have a personal assistant or carer, whether that be privately funded or given through social care. If you have access to this for limited hours, it will likely be of benefit for you to decide which tasks you struggle with most and work out how best to make the most of the hours you have.

If you don't have access to this, or you still need to do some aspects of these tasks by yourself, here are some ways you may be able to reduce stress on these tasks:

- Have your food shopping delivered to you, or if this is not possible, work out whether it is better to do smaller, regular shops or one bigger one each time.
- Set up direct debits for bill payments.
- Consider easier methods for tasks – such as getting a coverless duvet to reduce difficulty with changing bedding, or using laundry gel or tablets that you throw in with the clothes.
- If you have appointments that are re-occurring, try and have these at the same time or day of the week to lessen stress of forgetting them.

We also discussed in Chapter 2 specific tasks such as cooking and cleaning, which might also help you to navigate living independently.

You might experience homesickness or sadness at missing your old environment, your family or the different support you had. This is valid – make sure you are supporting yourself in any ways you need to help with this, like having phone calls with your family or bringing along photos or items from home.

Employment

Like education, not all chronically ill and autistic individuals can work, and that doesn't mean you are a failure or a bad person. Everybody is different – some can manage full-time work, some part-time, some a few hours and some none. It is all valid – as a disabled person, much of society and the working world is not set up for you, and that is not your fault.

However, if you are employed or wanting to be, this section will discuss how you can make this more accessible and tailored to you as an individual.

Applications and interviews

Most job application and interview processes are inaccessible for a variety of reasons, but employers are obligated to make adjustments for you as a disabled candidate if this is something you disclose. For example, you may be able to ask to:

- be given questions in advance so you can feel more prepared and less anxious
- have the interview in a sensory-friendly room, such as lower lighting and a quieter space
- submit the application or take a test in a different format, such as verbally or by video
- have additional time to complete tests and answer interview questions
- have the interview at a certain time of day.

In order to have these adjustments made to a recruitment process, disability charity Scope recommend that you:

- ask questions about the process surrounding your own needs, such as what the format will be, what the room is like, the length of the interview and whether there will be a test
- tell them the ways that the process is inaccessible, how you are disabled and what you need from them
- send an email so there is a written record of your request in case there are any problems
- try and come to a conclusion with them on alternatives if they refuse your adjustments
  - If this does not happen, you may want to report this and ask for advice. In the UK, this could mean contacting your Citizens' Advice Bureau, for example. Services vary by country, but if you're stuck for help, a local library may be a good place to start for support.[1]

Aside from adjustments made to the processes themselves, as an autistic person you may want to describe in advance any ways that you might communicate or engage differently. For example, some employers will look for active eye contact, which you may not be comfortable with.

Reasonable adjustments at work[2]

You are also entitled to having reasonable adjustments once you are in your job. These generally include changes to the workplace itself, equipment and processes, as well as accessible formats of information. For example:

- Changing the structure of the working day or allowing part-time work
- Adding a wheelchair ramp to the building
- Getting you adapted equipment, like a standing or ergonomic desk
- Allowing a support worker
- Changing the lighting in the building
- Placing you into a quieter room
- Allowing working from home
- Allowing time for treatments or more frequent breaks

Just like in the application process, if this is refused or a compromise can't be found, this can be classed as discrimination.

I started employment over a year ago after gaining the confidence to challenge the belief that I would never be able to hold down a job. It hasn't been easy. The workplace isn't built for my needs and getting reasonable adjustments has been essential. However, I am proud of the work that I do.

I've faced discrimination in the workplace before and it has affected my self-esteem. However, I'm starting to think that it says more about the organisation that you work for than it does about who you are as a person. We have a lot to offer in the world of employment, if only things were structured in a way for us to thrive without facing severe consequences to our health.

I've found that I don't have the same capacity for masking that I used to, which is both a negative and a positive. I stand out as 'the obvious one' amongst other autistic employees, which means that I can be treated differently in employment. I worry that this will impact my autistic colleagues and their willingness to unmask. Everyone should have a right to be themselves in the workplace. That includes when they are struggling and needing support. – **Eli**

Being in the workplace

If you are working in an office space or a similar environment, you might find it helpful to make adaptations to this yourself alongside any adjustments your employer makes with you. For example:

- Wearing ear defenders or listening to music
- Using sensory aids, both to regulate yourself and reduce symptoms like fatigue
- Having a space in the corner of an office or by a wall, or putting up screens, to reduce sensory input
- Using speech to text or reader software
- Asking colleagues to be clear with expectations and instructions
- Detailing your access needs in your email signature or automatic reply
- Having everything you need in reaching distance to reduce steps and transitions that need to be taken
- Asking for extra time to process or respond to information

If you work in a non-office space, there may be other adjustments you need to put in place. For example, if you work in hospitality or retail, you should be allowed adjustments such as taking short breaks if it gets overwhelming, or having music lowered. Shorter shifts may be helpful due to potential overwhelm and build-up of sensory needs.

> With work, I mask a lot. It is realistically hard for me to choose between not getting incomes vs. self-care when it comes to my disabilities. To me, work requires a high level of boundaries setting and strict micromanagements. Not when dealing with the work itself, but more with my personal routines before and after work hours.
>
> As an autistic person, my unmasked self could endanger my employment. I notice that I get hired much later than my neurotypical peers, perhaps from my upbringing and my presentation that sometimes aren't convincing that I have the skills that the employers need. – **MS**

Commuting can also be a difficult part of navigating employment, particularly if this has to be via public transport. It may be helpful to travel at off-peak times or get to work earlier to reduce the effect of a busy commute, and it can be helpful to use sensory aids and have an activity to do whilst commuting to minimise impact.

Working from home
Particularly since the start of the Covid-19 pandemic, many workers will now work from home. This can be very helpful to chronically ill and autistic individuals for a variety of reasons, such as the fact that you can create your own environments and use less energy on commuting or masking during conversations in the office. Some of the ways you can make working from home work for you could include:

- Knowing where you are going to work. We discussed in Chapter 4 that sometimes our beds can be the best places for us, but many autistic people also like to have a specific work environment to support transitions between work and home. This might be a desk space, your kitchen table or just another room in the house.
- Setting up your sensory environment to work for you. Do you need sensory aids nearby, different lighting, or any ways of setting up your space for easy access to documents? How can meetings become more accessible – do you need to set out instructions to your colleagues such as keeping themselves muted when they aren't speaking?
- Looking at how the work day needs to be set up for you to be able to transition between tasks and making sure your energy is used in a way that supports your needs. For example, do you find meetings easier in the morning or the afternoon? Do you need to block out specific hours to work on projects when you will have more energy? Does it help to start your day with a hard task to get it over with, or do you prefer to start with something gentle?

Alyson is an autistic 30-year-old who has asthma, a pituitary condition, migraines and PTSD. She said:

> It does make it very hard and emotionally draining to keep a job. I have an art therapist who helps me manage my stress, and process confusing/upsetting things which makes it easier for me to manage. A job where you have a supportive manager or are part of a team so when you are out you know that there are people covering for you is helpful, otherwise the stress of missing and coming back to tons of work makes it hard to take care of your needs. Being remote has

also dramatically changed my life and enabled me to keep a job longer than I have been able to in the past. I can be in my own comfortable environment and take breaks when I am overwhelmed, pet my dog or lay down if I need to. – **Alyson**

Freelancing

Many chronically ill and autistic people find that they struggle with traditional employment and can make self-employment or free-lancing work better for them. This could include anything from consultancy, to freelance journalism, to having a small business.

This sort of work can mean that you have a lot more flexibility to work the amount of hours that are accessible to you, at times accessible to you. It can also mean being able to work around medical appointments and treatments, as well as working in environments and with people that are accessible and effective for you. Many freelancers also work from home, so the environment is less stressful and you don't have to struggle with a commute.

Jasper is a self-employed freelancer. He said:

I can just tell people no if it isn't going to be how I want it to be and I have a strict procedure of how I do things. If they're hesitant I will decline because I need to look after my health first. Being self-employed means I don't have to worry about working from eight to six every day. I usually work hours I know I can work for me, which tends to be ten or eleven in the morning to slightly later in the afternoon. I also don't work every single day. If I have two or three things on one day I won't work the next day.

The majority of the people I work with are disabled themselves so we have open communication and make sure we're accessible to everyone. I have personal assistants that are suited to my work to help me.

It is worth pushing through and finding something you enjoy because otherwise I've personally found that in the long run it's actually worse for your health. – **Jasper**

Freelancing can have its challenges. It can mean that money is uncertain, and you don't have holiday or sick pay. You might struggle as an autistic person to manage finances, such as filing tax returns, so you may need to find support with this such as having a financial advisor or accountant available. Some people also feel lonely as you don't necessarily have access to the same level of community as you would working in an office, and this can be isolating and sometimes understimulating, so you might have to work harder to find these connections elsewhere if you don't already have them.

Caring for yourself after the work or school day

Everyone will have different needs following their work or school day, depending on their environment, the support they get and what sort of regulation they partake in. The stressors of these sorts of environments are going to be different for every chronically ill and autistic individual, so don't be worried if you find certain aspects of them easier or harder than another person, or if you have different needs in the period after you've left such an environment.

You might find that you need to put in a routine for after work to make sure that you are looking after yourself properly, such as making sure you have a snack, or putting in time to regulate sensory needs, do a small amount of exercise or decompress.

Things that might help you after school or work could include:

- Putting on comfier or sensory-friendly clothing
- Taking time out by yourself
- Making sure any needs around medication or treatment have been fulfilled – e.g. making sure you have eaten enough salt, drunk enough water, done a tube feed or changed any dressings
- Watching something comforting or listening to music or white/brown noise
- Icing or heating any painful areas of the body
- Having easy food available to you if it is a bad day, such as a ready meal or frozen food

These needs might also change from day to day, especially if you are in a role that doesn't have a specific structure or if you are freelancing on multiple projects, for example. If you have more meetings one day, you might need more time to yourself to decompress and stop masking, whereas if you have a day more to yourself working intensely on a project it may be that you have more needs around resting your body physically. This might be something that is trial and error, particularly if you are new to a job, so don't be concerned if this takes a while to work out.

Not defining yourself

Although I felt it was important to have a chapter all about education and employment as places that are extremely inaccessible and people often need support with, I want to end the chapter talking about the fact that life is not only about work and school.

I am redefining what success means to me by getting off the treadmill of education and work, instead focusing on learning to accept myself and live authentically as an autistic individual. This has been hard financially and is not possible for everyone, but I would encourage anyone who can to take a step back and evaluate what they need to live authentically and to enjoy life, rather than to keep pursuing goals that are based on the societal pressures of an allistic world. This will not stop others from being ableist towards you, or change society, but it will help you to rid yourself of internalised ableism and work towards a place of self-acceptance. – **Harriet**

If you as a disabled person cannot access these places, you are not a failure. It is not a moral failing to have to step back from work or education, whether temporarily or permanently.

If you can access these places, but can't go all the time or can't commit to them as much as you'd like, you're also not failing, you're not lazy or uncaring.

Whatever your status is with education and employment, you shouldn't define yourself by your engagement with them – that isn't healthy for anyone, whether they are disabled or not.

The society that we live in often defines us only by this, but we are more. We are our hobbies, specialist interests, passions, the love we give others and more besides.

I want that to be one of the main takeaways from this chapter.

KEY TAKEAWAYS FROM THIS CHAPTER

- Education and employment are spaces that are often inaccessible for a huge variety of reasons.

- There are lots of accommodations that can be made, but they still won't be accessible to everyone – you are not a failure.
- University provides lots of new and often unique challenges. It can take some time to get used to it and structure your life.
- Recruiters and employers are obligated to adjust inaccessible elements of processes, equipment and jobs.
- Sensory aids can be key to managing both your sensory input and your levels of fatigue whilst in education and employment.

6

Personal relationships

All kinds of relationships can be affected by your life as an autistic and chronically ill person, in plenty of different ways. These won't always be negative, but you may find that you have to navigate relationships differently or put in place different boundaries to others, for example.

I have struggled with relationships my whole life, both pre- and post-diagnosis as autistic, although being able to understand why I am the way I am made it feel more comfortable and less like I'm simply unlikeable or a failure.

Ultimately, you will find people who want to love you just as you are – and not just in the romantic sense. I didn't believe that when it was said to me, so I'm not expecting you to suddenly decide it's the truth – but it will happen. I think it often happens when you least expect it.

During this chapter we will discuss different kinds of personal relationships including friends, family and romantic relationships, and how they can be affected by being autistic and chronically ill.

Making friends

> The main advice I could give is to take your time and know that you don't need loads of friends to be happy and content. There are lots of good people out there though! – **Adam**

I found it really hard to make friends in school.

I wasn't interested in the same things as other kids, and I preferred being around adults or helping to look after other children. I didn't like the same games, and I was often found in the corner of the library instead of on the loud, bustling playground at lunchtimes.

I was bullied heavily for years and when I did make friends, it always seemed to go wrong. I wish I had known that I was just autistic, rather than broken.

When I became more chronically ill as I got further into the school system, it was also hard to ever make plans because I didn't know if I'd be able to go or not when the time came, and I was always missing school so I lost sense of the dynamics and inside jokes going on.

But really, I just wasn't around anyone who understood me – most of my closest friends now are disabled too in some way, so we understand each other better, or do the work to understand if we don't already.

For some autistic and chronically ill people, their autistic traits have impacted them throughout their whole life, whereas their chronic illnesses might have come later. This is the case for Lauren, as someone who has contracted long Covid:

I've been excluded many times over the years for things which I now realise were my autistic traits, and even as an adult I experience bullying for both being autistic and chronically ill. Being chronically ill means that people would rather pretend I don't exist, than make the very small effort to include me or even just talk to me. The loneliness I have felt in the past year has been crushing, because I know that I've not even done anything wrong to excuse people's behaviour. – **Lauren**

Some of the things that have helped me to find my people have included:

- Being around people with similar interests, for example at clubs and societies

It isn't always easy to do this, because of the anxiety of trying new things and meeting new people. But you might find that being around your special interest, for example, draws you to doing so, and you might meet others along the way.

This is something much more easily accessible if you are a university student, as you won't have to spend so much time trying to find societies or working out where they are, as groups are more likely to be actively recruiting members, and the details of different societies given out often. If you aren't a student though, many places have Facebook or Instagram pages that you can join or explore to learn more before you try going along.

If you don't want to go to anything in person, it's now quite easy to find similar communities through closed Facebook groups, Discord servers or platforms like TikTok and Twitter. Most of these platforms will have pages and groups for autistic people and chronically ill people, but also for all sorts of things that might include your special interests.

Online friendships are not a second best to in-person friendships, and can often be just as genuine a connection. Some of my best friends have been made online, and this is the case for many in the disabled community, particularly those who have struggled with being home or bedbound. Make sure to be safe, especially if considering meeting up in real life.

To start you off, you can find other autistic individuals using hash-tags like #ActuallyAutistic, #NeurodiverseSquad and #AutisticPride. For chronically ill people, you can try #NEISVoid, #pwME, #Chron-icallyIll and those of specific conditions, too. In Chapter 9, there is also a list of people I recommend you follow to start you off.

- Not expecting that everyone will understand me and my conditions

As I have become older, I have learnt that there are people out there who will not try and understand you as an autistic and chronically ill person. I no longer try and force myself to be around these sorts of people just because I want to have friends.

The people who truly love you and want to be in your life will make the effort to learn about your support needs, the ways you might communicate differently to them, or the fact that you hav-ing these conditions doesn't mean you don't want to be asked to go out.

- Knowing I don't need to have heaps of friends

I used to think that I had to have lots of friends, just because soci-ety tells us we should have loads of people around us. I have the people I need, and that's what matters.

I have people in my life who I don't see regularly or even text regularly, but I know that if I needed them tomorrow, they would be there for me without question. And that's hugely important to me as someone who struggles to communicate with loads of people all the time.

- Doing things I love, and not forcing myself to do things I don't

When I moved to university, my impulse was to try and do things I didn't want to do just to make friends. I don't really like clubbing and I only drink alcohol occasionally and socially, not only because of my chronic pain and noise sensitivities, but just because of the nature of my own hobbies. I found the people in my flat, on my course and in my societies who felt a similar way, and we do other activities together, like going to the theatre, going out for breakfast or having a couple of drinks in a calm, sensory-friendly environment.

You shouldn't feel like you have to do things you don't like just for the sake of a relationship – people who love you will understand your reasons, and won't take your decision not to participate personally.

I'm finding relationships to be the hardest part of unmasking. The friends I've made since diagnosis feel so different than my pre-diagnosis friends, because I am showing up differently now, and looking for something different in the people I spend time with. I've been learning to trust myself in terms of – is this a safe person to be around? And if they are not, I'm feeling ok to stay masked and not to get too deep into relationship with them.

When I first shared my autism diagnosis with some friends,

I had a few people tell me those dismissive things that many of us have heard – 'but you don't look autistic!' or 'Everyone's a little autistic!' or 'but you're funny!' I think it's caused some rifts in my friendships – partly because I am no longer participating in the contract we made when I was completely masked. I am asking more for what I need now, and it's not exactly what they signed up for originally, right? At that point I probably didn't even know what I needed, myself. Now I'm learning a lot more about what I need – as an autistic person AND as someone with colitis.

I'm taking to heart that adage – you can't change how people treat you, you can observe how they treat you and decide if you want to participate. – **Emily**

I'm a friend of a chronically ill autistic person – how can I help?

Many chronically ill and/or autistic people may feel guilty for not being available to hang out all the time, having to cancel or struggling to visit certain places. Some of the ways I've found that my friends can support me include:

- If we're making plans as a whole group, I always get to say whether a venue is okay for me first before any plan is set.
- Everyone invites me to things even if they think I'm likely to say no, to make sure I'm still included.
- They check if they can do anything to make something more accessible or support me to make things easier.
- Everyone knows what to do if I experience certain symptoms, such as if I feel like I might pass out, or have sensory overwhelm. To help them with this, I make sure I have all the equipment needed and let them know where key items are in my bag.

- We always go to restaurants that have my safe foods unless I request otherwise, and they don't make me feel awkward for needing that.
- They understand that sometimes plans will have to change.

Ultimately, that final point is one of the main ones for me – make sure your friend knows they are not an inconvenience for having support needs that you might not have.

These are things that can get easier with time, as people will get used to your needs and there will be less need to continually ask or check in. For example, two of my best friends are getting married next year, and they asked about my access needs to attend – but they had already guessed them and were just making sure!

It can take time to get to that point, though. They knew me for nearly three years before we got to this point where it is very natural to us. Sometimes you might find that friends get it wrong, and it can be worth working through this – it's often a genuine mistake and you can work with them to understand what went wrong and how they can include or support you better.

In any friendship, there will be separate needs that have to be thought about, differences between you in terms of communication that you have to remember, or compromises to be made. It just may be that these are different in a friendship to a chronically ill autistic person than they are within a friendship with someone else.

JJ spoke to me about losing friendships as a chronically ill autistic person. They said:

I've lost a lot of friendships because of being chronically ill. People commonly express sympathy and offer kindness and advice when they learn I'm ill, but after weeks or months or years when they realise I'm not going to 'get well soon' they often get angry or frustrated with me, blaming me or implying that I like being ill and I'm not trying to get better. I think this comes from fear. People want to believe that their health is a thing they can control, and when they're presented with someone who is ill and stays ill despite doing 'all the right things', this belief is challenged, which makes them uncomfortable. – **JJ**

Be patient with disabled friends in your life and understand that they are not being difficult, and it isn't that they don't appreciate you if they seem like they are not invested in you. They might be struggling to have the energy to engage in conversation or events, or might have too many things happening, causing overwhelm.

Relationships with your family

Not only can being a chronically ill autistic person impact friendships, but it can impact your family relations too.

Some of my friends and family members are still on the fence about me living as a chronically ill and autistic person, in the sense that they don't try to understand when I'm having an issue, even when it's very obvious (physically showing and or with genuine proof). Or just admitting in general that I am indeed different and have different needs. I feel like relationships are transactional and unforgiving. – **MS**

Family members are often the people you see the most, and whilst some may be your biggest advocates, others may not understand you, and some may find it really difficult to process their feelings about what you are facing.

If you are someone who has become chronically ill later in life, or perhaps you have deteriorated, you might find that there is an element of grief that your family members feel – for you, but perhaps also for themselves and what your relationship looks like.

Sometimes, family members can also feel a variety of emotions wondering whether your conditions are genetic or hereditary, worrying they are at fault, for example. Some parents might feel responsible or might feel guilty that they should have spotted signs or traits earlier, such as autistic traits in childhood. For some, it might also mean learning they too are autistic or chronically ill, so they will be on their own journey, too.

The first thing to say is that it is not your responsibility to process and comprehend those feelings for them. The grief that can come with chronic illness – of feeling like there are things you can no longer do, or like you are different to your peers, or any number of other things – is something that you may feel, and it can be difficult enough for you to process that within yourself. You can support them, and may want to discuss it, but it is ultimately something they need to come to terms with on their own.

Grief is not a linear journey – we know this when it comes to the death of someone we love, as we talk about the variety of emotions that can occur throughout, whether that be denial, anger or sadness. This, for some, is exactly the same with chronic illness.

You might find that not every person in your family understands what you experience or how it affects your life. This could manifest in a couple of different ways, which can all be difficult to manage for different reasons:

- Sadness or upset – in a selfish way that you can't do

what they want you to do anymore, or simply sadness
for you
- Denial – believing that you are exaggerating or it's not
  possible that you're experiencing what you are
- Being pushy and trying to make you do things that you
  can't

> I think being a Black woman there are a lot of narratives
> around being strong, independent, and suffering through
> pain as a badge of honour. I did this for many years and
> could not understand why it was so hard for me. I put these
> expectations on myself and everyone else had them too, so
> asking for help was almost impossible. There is also a lot
> of stigma around mental health within the Black commu-
> nity. My parents took most of my physical concerns seri-
> ously (migraines, asthma, pituitary condition, etc.) but
> when it came to the social anxiety, feeling burnt out and
> 'Depressed', the meltdowns – all of that just was not talked
> about or brushed off. One time a doctor mentioned I could
> be depressed and my dad said 'no' and that was the end of
> it. – **Alyson**

It can be particularly difficult for family members to understand if
they have not encountered autism or chronic illness in their lives
before, or if they have had ableism taught to them by others (or
indeed society, as we will discuss later, in Chapter 7).

Unfortunately, with family there is not a singular solution as their
reasons for struggling with your disabilities can be extremely
variable.

Sometimes it may help if you provide them information from charities or official organisations that they can see as legitimate. Open

discussions about your conditions and stigmas around them can also be helpful.

Not everyone is open to being educated, and that can be more difficult for you. You might feel unsupported or like you don't have anyone in your family who understands. You are not alone in this and it might be helpful to engage with others who are similar to you, as we've discussed in the friendship part of this chapter.

When it comes to discussing your needs, it might be helpful not to refer to the conditions themselves at all, as the focus on 'labels' can sometimes be what some people have an issue with. It may be more helpful to say 'I need the lights to be turned down' rather than attributing this to your autism or your chronic illness, for example.

Relationships with siblings

Relationships with siblings of any age can be particularly unique when you are disabled.

Sometimes it can be more difficult because you need more attention or support, and this can impact them. My siblings are all younger than me, and have had difficulties sometimes in the past with feeling like I was getting more attention whilst I was in hospital or when I was having a flare-up.

It has helped to talk to them about what is going on, which is in the next part of the chapter. I like to spend time with them when I can and my parents also make sure that time is spent with them where needed, and we have had discussions in the past about the fact that they are just as loved. All of my siblings are also neurodivergent, so it can be difficult for their needs to be balanced.

Sometimes siblings may become part of those caring for you. This will be different for everyone – some might find this difficult or feel guilty, whereas for others it will work well due to your relationship.

Some areas have support networks or groups for siblings of disabled people.

Talking to young family members

One of the hardest parts of family relations and disability, for me, has always been talking to younger family members. I have three younger siblings, and they've all had varying levels of awareness of my chronic illnesses as they've grown.

When we explained my collagen disorder to my sister when she was very young, she ended up telling people for several years that I had 'wobbly bones' – whilst inaccurate, it worked for her to understand why I couldn't be as rough-and-tumble as others, and why I used a mobility aid. Different things work for different kids!

Some kids might find metaphors helpful – for example, the spoon or battery theories we discussed back in Chapter 4, on pacing, may be useful. Others may prefer to be told about the practicalities of what is different about your body and brain compared to theirs.

Kids tend to be quite malleable. I've not often come across a child who doesn't accept me for who I am, whether that be kids I work with in volunteering settings, or kids I meet in public. It doesn't tend to bother them – but they do tend to be quite inquisitive.

When it comes to autism, this can be harder to explain as although some of our traits have external presentations like meltdowns or stimming, much of what we experience is internal. This is particularly true of things that kids might impact on, like sensory overwhelm building up.

The way I've tended to explain much of this is in terms of my needs and what they can do to help me rather than how autism works, as this is often less difficult for them to process. For example, I might talk about how bright lights and loud noises can make me very anxious and overwhelmed, and describe that if I get overwhelmed it can help me to move somewhere else, to turn the lights off, or to turn down any music. Again, every child is different, and some may ask about the 'why' – especially those who are in that particular phase of growing up!

I'm the family member of a chronically ill autistic person – what can I do to help?

A lot of the ways you can support your family member are the same as those previously listed in this chapter for friends of chronically ill people, but here are some extra ways that might be applicable in the home setting:

- Don't push them to be a part of family activities for the sake of appearance or routine – if they are saying they aren't well enough, believe them.
- Don't be angry if they aren't contributing to chores or errands even if they previously could – most of us wish for nothing more than to be able to help out.
- Ask them about the small things that can help them to live comfortably at home – sometimes there are specific issues in a home setting that contribute to both our chronic illness symptoms or to our difficulties, and these might be very small changes you can make as a family.
- Help them make sure they are hydrated and nourished – there are a variety of traits of both autism and chronic illnesses that can make us less likely to eat and drink, from interoception which we discussed in Chapter 1 to our rest patterns going over mealtimes. Prompts or bringing us food and drink can go a long way to combat this.
- Allow plans to be moved around if needed, and don't be angry at the need for this.

Navigating romantic relationships

A romantic relationship as a chronically ill autistic person can be something difficult to navigate for a variety of reasons. While you may want to be with someone you might find that, for example:

- your support needs and symptoms mean you can't easily date or have the time to put what you want into a relationship
- it is hard to find someone who will understand and accommodate your needs
- you find it hard to trust people you don't know.

Whilst there is no simple answer to any of these situations, and they are entirely personal, it has to be said that dating as a chronically ill autistic person is not impossible if it's something you want to do.

You are not unlovable because you are a chronically ill and autistic individual. You are not difficult for having certain needs in a relationship that other people do not have.

You do not deserve less for being who you are. You deserve fulfilling, understanding, reciprocated, loving relationships – and that goes for both romantic love and any other kind that we might or might not have touched on during this chapter.

> I think connecting with other neurodivergent people is important. I've always had an easier time making friends with people with ADHD, ASD or OCD, and wondered why that was until I was diagnosed. It's important to have people you can unmask around. My spouse is allistic, but has OCD, and they appreciate my infodumps and my 'quirks'. They also have Crohn's disease among other gastrointestinal

disorders, and they were very helpful when I was navigating my own GI complaints. I don't know how I would have managed my burnouts without my partner's support. They also help me interface with physicians and manage my many medications for me, which takes a huge burden off of my shoulders. – **Dylan**

A note on sexuality

Did you know that autistic people are more likely to be LGBTQ+ (lesbian, gay, bisexual, trans, queer, questioning, pansexual, or any other sexuality or gender identity that is not cisgender, heterosexual or heteroromantic)?

This is sometimes something that chronically ill and/or autistic people do not get to explore because they are focused on managing, learning about or accepting their conditions.

If this sounds like you, and it's something you'd like to think about in more detail, here are some recommendations for books about or that discuss sexuality (and gender) that might be helpful:

- *Queerly Autistic: The Ultimate Guide for LGBTQIA+ Teens on the Spectrum* by Erin Ekins (2021)
- *Queer Body Power* by Essie Dennis (2022)
- *Unmasking Autism* by Dr Devon Price (2022)

If you are LGBTQ+, being a chronically ill autistic can make it harder to access spaces made for the community as they are often in loud, busy spaces, or only in physical environments like bars. Pride parades can be hard to manage too. A couple of ways to get involved can be:

- Engaging with the communities on social media, whether

that be publicly or in closed Facebook or messaging groups
- Community initiatives that are making space for queer people outside of bars, such as Canny Queer Collective in Newcastle
- Meeting up with a smaller group of friends who you relate to
- Seeing if your city has any spaces like LGBTQ+ cafes or bookshops
- Creating your own noise like writing a blog or creating content

You might also find that as a disabled LGBTQ+ person, you face being desexualised or told you can't know your own sexuality or romantic orientations both by others in the community or those in spaces like healthcare.

This might make you feel uncomfortable to seek out connections. You deserve to feel comfortable in yourself and whilst it may take time, you do know yourself better than anyone else.

It might become a case of experimenting with labels or with dating – remember that you can always change label or realise that something isn't for you, it's a process!

Dating and the early stages – telling people about your conditions

It isn't as simple as just saying 'I'm autistic and chronically ill', is it? There can be a number of things to think about... will they understand? Will they suddenly believe we could never work due to biases they already have? Am I in a safe place to tell them if something happens? When do I tell them?

All of this can be different in every single situation with every different person you come across, and that can make life really difficult.

Whilst I can't give a step-by-step guide on this one, here are some questions to consider about how and when you could bring up your conditions:

- If you are using a dating app, do you want to make them part of your profile or early conversations?
  You might find that this more quickly weeds out those who have prejudices, but may also lead to some hateful messages. Whether you do this may depend on whether you believe you could handle any negativity like this. If you are visibly disabled, for example, you might have no choice but for your disability to be on display – in this case, make sure you are reporting and blocking anyone who sends abuse your way.
- Are they trying to meet you somewhere that isn't accessible, and are you pushing yourself too far for appearances' sake?
  If you are physically going on a date, you shouldn't force yourself to go somewhere that isn't accessible for the sake of the other person. This doesn't mean you have to tell them about your conditions before meeting if that makes you uncomfortable, but could you ask to meet somewhere quieter, closer or that you already know is accessible and supportive to your needs?
- Do you want to tell them in person or would you feel more comfortable discussing it over text (for example)?
  For some autistic and disabled people, face-to-face discussions may not be preferable. You might decide that it is easier to have important conversations like this in a way that is friendlier to your needs. Communicating over text or by any other means of conversation doesn't devalue what you are saying, similar to how we discussed AAC and communication needs in Chapter 1.

Not everyone is going to understand what autism or a chronic illness is, or know about your specific chronic illness. You might find it helpful to have something planned to provide some context and think about questions the person might have for you about it.

I'm dating a chronically ill autistic person – what can I do to help?

You know how some people say that a relationship is two halves coming together?

For many autistic and chronically ill individuals, our relationships need to be an additional part of our life, not something that replaces any of our other needs, supports or parts of ourselves.

You might find that as a relationship with a chronically ill autistic person goes on, you are more in tune with some of their needs or you become a bigger part of this support – but in the early days, it is unlikely they will want you to try and take over any of this.

There are some ways you can be helpful and supportive in these early days, such as:

- Ask about their communication needs – do they ever have times where they might need to communicate through text, written word or text-to-speech software? Remember that these other ways of communicating do not mean they are less interested – they are simply aids.
- Ask about their accessibility needs – do they need to be in a quiet space, a place that doesn't have stairs to get inside, or somewhere that is very aware of allergens, for example? Disabled people can have extremely varying needs even if they have the same disability, so you should always check!
- Don't be offended if they cancel – it's probably not about you! When you're disabled, even the best laid plans or things we're most excited about might not be viable once we come to the day because of how we're feeling or symptoms that might have come up.

- Learn more about their conditions – think about following disability advocates or content creators (there's a list at the back of this book!) or reading up on their conditions. When disabled people have to educate you, it can take a lot of energy needed for other things, and it can be helpful if you are curious and start learning.

Relationships, love and care

As a chronically ill autistic person in a long-term relationship, you might find that there is a very fine balance to strike between wanting to keep hold of some ways of caring for yourself, and your partner wanting to do them as an act of love. It can take a while to balance this.

This will be different for everyone. Some romantic partners will have one of them acting as a carer for the other, and there's nothing wrong with that if it is what works for you as a pair. It doesn't make you a burden or mean that you have 'nothing to contribute' to the partnership, which are both stereotypes that couples including a carer have often faced in the media.

Here are some small ways that a partner could show care and love for an autistic and chronically ill partner:

- Filling up your water bottle
- Carrying an emergency salty snack for you
- Making sure to ask before they touch you, as you might be in pain or be in sensory overwhelm
- Helping you move out of noisy environments
- Checking in that you've taken your meds
- Helping you find somewhere to sit down

All of these are things you might not like someone to do, because you want to be more independent or don't need them, or you may want them to do more. I would recommend having discussions with partners about what might be a boundary or not, so that neither of you are feeling anxious or awkward about what is wanted or not.

Sex and disability

Whilst as a sex-repulsed asexual person I can't talk from experience in this part of the chapter, I still think it's hugely important to discuss how being autistic and chronically ill can affect sex and sexual relationships. I asked some of the contributors to tell me about how this affects their experience of sex and relationships.

Meg told me about their experience of sex and its interconnectedness with romantic relationships, and said:

Media constantly perpetuates the idea that people in romantic relationships have the perfect life – constantly having sex and barely able to keep their hands off each other, have the energy to go on dates and getaways whenever the mood strikes them, and have weddings last minute with their closest friends. It isn't like that for me, and I assume for a lot of chronically ill autistic people. For me, I not only don't have the physical energy for sex, but I get overwhelmed by touch and sounds so easily it makes it difficult to be intimate. I've been with my partner for four years, who is also neurodivergent and understands what it is like to be overwhelmed in a sensory sense, but it does have an impact on our overall relationship. I can't go on spontaneous dates without having a meltdown – I need to know where we're going, how long we're going there for and what to expect from that experience. I'm also not well enough to leave the house a lot of the time. It makes me feel like I'm letting my partner down because I have to have things so carefully planned, and even then we have to cancel plans when I'm not well enough to do anything. It makes things incredibly difficult.

That being said, I'm incredibly grateful I have a partner who is open and understanding, maintains great communication with me and understands my physical and mental cues better than I do myself. He takes care of me and I take care of him – we understand each other, and I would say he is the only person in my life who truly understands what it is like to be a chronically ill autistic person (or at least, be in a relationship with one!). – **Meg**

It's multifactorial. My libido is practically non-existent most of the time, it's too overwhelming to engage in intimacy beyond skin to skin cuddling or superficial kissing. Luckily my husband is okay with this. – **Chey**

It is a different experience. Being autistic makes me hypersensitive to my sensory needs, which include sexual preferences. And being chronically ill also has its own difficulties with physical limitations.

I often found myself to have very different preferences and boundaries than people I was intimate with (in regards of romantic or sexual relationships). And it eventually became an issue because sometimes, what I'm okay and not okay with when it comes to sex and relationships were bothering to the other person.

One simple example is that I wipe my mouth after kissing, because I don't like the lingering feeling of saliva on my skin. It was offensive to some of my sexual/romantic partners.

And eventually it became an issue and a reason to start an argument.

It makes sexual and relationship experiences rather unpleasing and embarrassing at times. – **Anon**

Thinking about independence

Independent (adjective): not requiring or relying on something else; not requiring or relying on others (as for care or livelihood).[1]

That's not so simple when you're disabled, is it?

If I'm being honest, I don't think *anyone* is independent to the extent of the dictionary definition – everyone has needs of some sort that mean they rely on people or objects for something.

But for us, as autistic and chronically ill people, this is even more true – whether that be needing carers or having people in our life do certain tasks for us, needing mobility or other disability aids to live our lives as well as we can or having to use the welfare and benefits systems.

There is nothing wrong with this, and it is not something to be ashamed of.

Some of you may be wanting to find more independence, or might be pushed by professionals towards doing more yourself. Sometimes this is appropriate and useful, and sometimes it isn't. That is not for me to tell you.

If you need someone to perform daily tasks for you, to make sure you have taken your medication, to cook for you, or to help with any other task – you are not a failure.

What you might find, however, is that you don't want certain people in your life to perform certain tasks. For example, you might not want a partner to do this as you would lose that support if you separated, or you might not want your mum to do it because you want to move out eventually.

Not everyone has the privilege of accessing external carers or disability support, but you might want to see if there are things you can access to support you with these needs. If you can't access anything, you could consider thinking about the support you need and who or what can help with this, and whether this is right for you.

Knowing your worth

One of the biggest things I want to express in this chapter is that I want you to be able to feel supported and loved for who you are.

You can't always choose the people you are around, of course, especially when it comes to family – but where possible, you deserve to be around the people who make you feel good.

Good friends, partners and family won't make you feel like a burden, an inconvenience or like you are annoying them.

Being yourself when you don't feel accepted by society is much easier said than done, and will probably take time. You can read more about self-love and disability pride in Chapter 9 – but for this chapter, remember that those who truly love and support you will do so without pushing these negative feelings onto you.

You are no less worthy a human being for being disabled, and for many of us, our worth partially lies in being who we are because it is a part of our personality, the way we look at society in different ways, educating people, working against an ableist society and more.

If people are not supportive of you, or are making you feel any of the negative emotions previously mentioned, you might first want to discuss this with them as they might not have realised that their words or actions were coming across in this way.

If it has not been a misunderstanding, you may find it necessary to set boundaries around your relationship if you feel like it is safe for you to do so. For example:

- You do not make me feel safe and comfortable, so I no longer want to spend time with you.
- I do not want to attend family events if [person] is also there, because they make me feel like I am inconvenient to the rest of the family.
- I feel like I can't be myself with you, so I don't think this relationship is right for me anymore.

KEY TAKEAWAYS FROM THIS CHAPTER

- You can find fulfilling and loving friendships and relationships as a chronically ill autistic person, and you truly deserve these.
- Your support needs matter – you shouldn't let these go for other people's convenience.
- Being 'independent' is almost a myth, and needing help from those around you is not a personal failing.
- You are so full of worth and you are not a burden.

7

Experiencing ableism

As an autistic and chronically ill individual, it is almost certain that ableism will have some impact on your life, and this comes in multiple different forms. As we will go on to discuss, there are several types of ableism and they sometimes intertwine with each other, or you may experience them independently of anyone or anything else.

Some of the chapters previous to this one in the book have talked about the ways ableism can impact us, for example if we don't have access needs met for us in school or work, but there are also a lot of other ways that ableism can come up for us.

What is ableism?

You get used to death threats and hate crimes really quickly. You get used to people calling you names or giving you nicknames, and then there's the more colloquial ableism like 'do you have a licence for that thing'. I don't have a licence, but I'd love to see them get up a hill with it. The media have perpetuated the idea that all disabled people are scrounging but it's so hard to get any benefits or support – I'm on my third round. It hasn't helped social perceptions of us. – **Alice**

Ableism (noun): policies, behaviours, rules, etc. that result in unfair or harmful treatment of disabled people (= people who have an illness, injury, or condition that makes it difficult for them to do things that most other people can do) and in a continued unfair advantage to people who are not disabled.[1]

It has also been defined as 'discrimination in favour of non-disabled people'. Sometimes you will also hear 'disablism' used, which is a similar term which places emphasis on the discrimination being against disabled individuals.

It's a bit more complicated than any of these definitions give credit for, though – there are multiple forms of ableism that disabled people are facing daily, which often layer on top of each other and can become significantly difficult to navigate. Ableism can not only have an impact on disabled people's mental health, but it can also impact how they can live their lives, the healthcare they receive and their access to a community.

Common types of ableism you may come across

Casual ableism

Casual ableism is what you might see from your average person, perhaps particularly on social media or when you try and explain your difficulties. This can stem from society's stereotypes about disability, and bad media representation.

Examples can include:

- 'But you don't look autistic'
- 'You're faking'
- 'That wheelchair user just got up'
- 'You just want special treatment'
- 'You should just try yoga and vitamins'

Lateral ableism

Lateral ableism refers to ableism that disabled people receive from other disabled people – this could be from someone who has a different type of disability, or it could be someone with the same condition believing you should be having the same experience they are. Many disabled people believe they cannot be ableist, but this is inaccurate and a common issue amongst disabled communities.

This can sometimes include backlash for using disability accommodations or aids, like a Blue Badge for disabled parking.

Examples can include:

- 'If I can do that, so can you'
- 'You're not as disabled as I am'
- 'You shouldn't be taking up those resources, we need them more'
- 'That's not a real disability'

Medical ableism

Medical ableism is unfortunately deeply rooted in the medical system and is faced by many. Long-term disabilities and health conditions are not taken seriously for many years, with some chronic illnesses taking years to be diagnosed – such as endometriosis taking an average of eight years in the UK.[2] Many may be denied testing or a diagnosis due to belief that someone is coping, and many autistic people will be told there is no 'proper reason' for a diagnosis.

Examples can include:

- 'It's all in your head'
- 'Mobility aids mean you're giving up on yourself'
- Being denied medication due to 'risk of addiction'
- Fat disabled people being told their problems are only due to their weight

- Being denied support because you appear to be 'coping'
- Use of the medical model and being focused on cures
- Disabled people being told not to have children
- Not being referred for a diagnosis without a 'valid reason'

Systemic ableism

Systemic ableism is the way that society places ableism onto disabled people through its institutions, policies and values. This could include through governmental policy and how the welfare state runs, how police perceive disabled people, and how legislation or institutions may not be supportive to disabled individuals.

Examples can include:

- Denial of benefits for 'looking well' or 'not being disabled enough'
- Schools and universities not providing support
- The Human Rights Act 1998 in the UK being violated
- Buildings still not having ramps or lifts
- Policemen finding disabled people 'suspicious'

Common ableism you might face as an autistic and chronically ill person

There are often common tropes that different groups of disabled people face. These tend to have been ingrained into people from the media, whether that be the representation of those conditions in television shows and films, or articles within journalism made to make disabled people the enemy.

You might find that stereotyping or discrimination against chronically ill autistic people might cause you to face:

- attitudes of belief that autism needs a cure or that you should be forced to mask or hide your autistic traits

- attitudes that chronically ill people aren't trying hard enough, are lazy or are faking
- beliefs that 'everyone is a little bit autistic' and this affecting whether or not you are given accommodations or support
- people believing doctors or professionals over your own lived experience
- lack of support for alternative forms of communication or AAC
- judgement around use of medications.

MS talked about the intersection of disability and race, and where it can contribute to ableism:

I am Southeast Asian, living in Indonesia. This is a place where ableism is encouraged heavily while basic (and various) knowledge is limited, especially knowledge about physical and mental health, and neurodiversity. I struggle a lot with my daily life, and I couldn't find a reliable source – let alone accommodation – to improve my situation, so I am pessimistic about life in general.

I do feel glad for being able to speak English, because from that, I could try to find information about self-care and life quality improvement from different sources. However, witnessing a lot of chronically ill and/or autistic people here who don't have the same privilege as me is rather painful. It gives me the feeling of frustration and despair from wanting to help, but also I don't feel like I have the mental capacity to do it alone.

Racial prejudice and favouritism are also a big issue. From an Asian (particularly Southeast Asian) perspective, which favours uniformity, it's very hard for people around to understand differences. It is as if neurodiversity with its uniqueness, as well as the concept of disabilities, are only Caucasians and Western people's experience (at least from my country's perspective). If we were to speak up about ourselves regarding this, we would be seen as weak and a misfit, or a major attention seeker. Which cause us to further be discriminated. It is a strange experience for me personally. It also doesn't help that so far, the media representation from my race is very minimal (if non-existent) regarding the topic. – **MS**

How to handle ableism from other people

There is unfortunately no single way to handle ableism, even within one specific form of it. You may find that your ability to handle it changes over time, or depends on whether you are in a good place or not. For me, if I am in pain, particularly fatigued or experiencing sensory overload, I am less able to process or handle ableism. I particularly experience more internalised ableism in those moments, too.

If you experience forms of ableism that are placed on you by other people, it is up to you as to whether you want to respond or challenge these.

Whilst you may feel responsible for breaking down other people's ableism, it is not your responsibility alone to stop ableism if you are already at your capacity or just trying to survive. If it comes from family or friends, it might feel too difficult to try and challenge it due to the relationships you have. You should not feel guilty for this – it is society's fault, not yours, and whilst you might want to try, it is okay if you can't.

However, if you do want to challenge casual or lateral ableism if you find yourself being spoken to or dealt with in an ableist way, you may want to work out how is best for you to do so. For some people, they may find they have 'stock responses' to ableism, which can mean it doesn't take as much capacity to respond as it is ready prepared. You don't have the responsibility to educate people, but you may want to. You might want a short or simple response that shuts it down, or may want to engage in conversation. This is up to you.

> Ableism has felt particularly present for me recently. I've been excluded and treated differently in services, workplaces and personal relationships. It has been present since I was a child, but the neurotypical, able-bodied adult world is a real nightmare to navigate.
>
> At first, I was quite passive and didn't stand up for myself. However, being around a community of other disabled people has helped me fight for my rights. My job is working with other autistic people and often supporting their rights. I would be a hypocrite if I didn't self-advocate but told the people I work with that they should. So, I've been pointing out when things aren't fair and have sought support from advocacy organisations. It is tiring though and you really need to make sure that you take time for your wellbeing. When it comes to fighting against ableism, rest is revolutionary. – **Eli**

Just as Eli says, one of the main factors when it comes to handling ableism can be the self-care you do. Whether you're an advocate coming up against ableism as part of your work, or just someone whose video has ended up on the wrong side of TikTok, ableism is absolutely exhausting. Remember to look after yourself, take time out and make sure you are using your support networks or sensory regulation techniques so that it doesn't become too over-whelming or damaging.

Where ableism intersects with other forms of discrimination, such as racism or homophobia, it can feel lonely or make it more difficult to handle. Dan said:

A lifetime of being subject to model minority ideals, being pressured to assimilate in order to be accepted and avoid discrimination in Western society, has severely damaged my ability to advocate for myself, including in healthcare settings.

It can get lonely living at the intersections of my racism and ableism, combined with all the other facets of my life. It's natural to want to be understood, and I often feel misunderstood even in chronically ill and autistic spaces, because there is often a lacking dimension regarding one of the significant facets of my life, such as my racial heritage. I hope to connect with more autistic and chronically ill people of colour in the coming years. It is of course important to respect our differences, and I'm never going to find someone with all the exact same experiences as me who will innately understand me completely, without issue. Communication is essential, and only with it can we undergo the mortifying ordeal of being known, and the reward of being loved. But of course, we tend to seek out those like us, not in exclusivity but in inclusion as a part of our lives. There are some things that we need to be able to talk about with those who live at the same intersections. – **Dan**

As Dan says, it can help to be around others who have similar experiences. There are groups and charities that support those with intersecting experiences or identities, such as Chronically Brown, who support disabled Asian people.

You might experience some forms of ableism on social media more prominently, if you engage with them publicly as a disabled person. You might find that you receive casual ableism, bullying or harassment on social media from strangers, or may experience lateral ableism from other disabled people online. In these cases, remember to use functions such as muting, blocking and reporting, and do not feel pressure to share any details or diagnoses that you do not want to.

There can be differences between responding to casual or lateral ableism as compared to medical or systemic ableism which impacts how you live your life or what you can access. In some cases, it might be appropriate to make reports to appropriate safeguarding or advocacy departments. Sometimes, it might be to an extent that it has to go to court or tribunal, for example. Medically, it may be necessary to get a second opinion.

Chey is a chronically ill and autistic nurse, and they spoke about how they navigate lateral ableism at work:

I see this almost daily. It is my mission to help people understand others' lived experiences so that we can progress and uplift everyone together... Where someone else may be enacting ableism I consider whether their...

- ...behaviour could be linked to their ADHD?
- ...anger could be linked to their pain?
- ...frustration is lack of access to this area?

Could it help if...

- …we gave them something to do, like a wordsearch or Rubik's cube?
- …I check they aren't due more pain relief? Maybe they need a Pain Specialist.
- …I review their medications?
- …we let them use the staff entrance to maintain their comfort and safety? – **Chey**

Gaslighting

Ableism, particularly medically, often takes the form of gaslighting.

Gaslighting refers to psychological treatment of someone that causes them to question their thoughts, their perception of reality or their memories.[3]

Disabled people are often treated this way when their disabilities, symptoms or difficulties are called into question and not believed. It can often be the case that the medical system pushes a disabled person from doctor to doctor, not knowing how to help or not believing you need help. This can lead us to question whether what we are experiencing is real at all.

Alongside questioning yourself, you might find it significantly more difficult to attend medical appointments or worry about whether something much more serious is wrong.

Some examples of this can include:

- Having your memories questioned
- Being told you have gotten ideas from the internet or that you don't know what you're talking about

- Being dismissed or told you are overreacting
- Having physical symptoms be attributed to your autism or to mental health difficulties like anxiety or depression
- Having symptoms attributed only to weight

Medical gaslighting appears particularly in women and people of colour. We will discuss this in more detail in Chapter 8.

Keeping symptom logs, recording what happens in your appointments, and taking someone with you or requesting an advocate to be present are ways you can try to prevent this and support your mental health when it occurs. If someone can't come with you, you might want to have debriefs with someone trusted as soon as you can after appointments, before you forget or mix up what might have happened.

Gaslighting may not always be on purpose, but it is still classed as abusive and/or neglectful if it occurs.

Internalised ableism

A unique form of ableism that many of us face, often without realising, is internalised ableism. This is because as disabled people we have been brought up in an ableist society, meaning that even though we are disabled ourselves, we may have internalised harmful or damaging beliefs about disability. This can be a very difficult thing to unlearn and process, and we often will not recognise or realise we are struggling with it.

Examples can include:

- Refusing treatment because we believe we should just get better
- Struggling to identify as disabled due to the stigma attached (rather than personal preference)

- Not using aids and accommodations so that we don't seem 'weak' or like we are 'failing'
- Believing that you should be able to do something because someone else with your condition can do it
- Having ableist thoughts when you see another disabled person doing it, due to your own beliefs about how they should be acting or handling themselves as a disabled person

> I think I have a lot of internalised ableism because I went undiagnosed until adulthood. So after 30 years of hearing people tell me to try harder, or tough it out, or that I am being dramatic, I still have a lot of those narratives in my head. I think practising self-compassion and creating new narratives or affirmations has helped me to unlearn that.
> – **Alyson**

There are a few ways that we can try to begin to unpick our internalised ableism, such as:

- Following disabled people on social media and watching good media representations of disabled people, to reinforce that disability is not a bad or shameful thing
- Beginning to take up more support and accommodations
- Questioning yourself when ableist thoughts and ideas pop up
- Helping your friends and family to process these ideas too, as they may be reinforcing them

This is unlikely to be a quick process. I've known I was disabled for quite a few years now, but it's something I still catch myself experiencing. But, it is extremely important to recognise and work on as it can cause you to struggle more than you need to by not having support, or becoming caught up in feeling like you should be getting 'better' when you can't do so.

There is often a high level of guilt that comes with internalised ableism, particularly that which might pop up in thoughts about another disabled person. If you are recognising it and working on it, you should give yourself kindness about this. It isn't your fault – it's the product of an ableist society, pressing these beliefs into us every single day.

> I experience ableism internally all the time. I frequently have a small inside voice telling me that I'm faking for attention or I'm not as disabled as I say I am, and this is most likely internalised from childhood experiences. But I have to take time to trust myself and remember my worst days that prove this voice wrong. – **Lauren**

Media representation and links to ableism

Unfortunately, the media – including everything from newspapers and factual programmes on the TV or radio all the way to fictional TV and film – has a lot to answer for when it comes to ableism towards disabled individuals.

There is not very much representation of individuals who are both autistic and chronically ill, which may impact the ways that many non-disabled people perceive that people can't have multiple disabilities. However, both autism and chronic illnesses have had some terrible representation that perpetuates some of the ableism we have already discussed in this chapter.

Much of mainstream media will reinforce ideas such as chronically ill people being lazy or autistic people needing a cure, or will publicise young people having meltdowns, for example. It can be very hard for us to watch and can affect our self-esteem, make us feel like we are lying or overreacting, and affect our relationships with others due to what they have seen and heard.

It can help to make sure that you have consumed some positive and affirming pieces of media to understand yourself better and remember that not everything in the media is accurate. Some positive representations of autism and chronic illness in media include:

- *Heartbreak High* (2022 reboot) – TV
- *A Kind of Spark* by Elle McNicoll (2021) – middle grade fiction
- *The Secret of Haven Point* by Lisette Auton (2022) – middle grade fiction
- Various books by Holly Smale, such as the Geek Girl series (2013–2017) – young adult fiction
- Fern Brady in Season 14 of *Taskmaster* (2022) – TV show
- The Brown Sisters series by Talia Hibbert (2019–2021) – adult fiction

KEY TAKEAWAYS FROM THIS CHAPTER

- There are multiple types of ableism you might face, and there are likely to be different ways you handle them.
- There is no shame in needing to seek support with handling ableism you have faced, whether it be professional or with those you know and love.
- There is also no shame in having internalised ableism to unpick, unlearn and understand. It's been ingrained in us by society and that isn't simple to undo.
- There are positive pieces of media out there and it can help to watch or read them to see yourself represented.

8

Gender, medical misogyny and menstrual health

As someone who presents in healthcare settings as female and is non-binary, I have long experienced the effects of medical misogyny throughout my journey – and it was a huge contributor to why I struggled to be diagnosed or given any support for as long as I was.

In a world where women and those assigned female at birth have been seen throughout history as hysterical – the world literally deriving from the Greek for 'uterus'[1] – there is no surprise this is a part of my experience and that of thousands of others when it comes to chronic pain, chronic illness and neurodivergence.

Pain in misogyny-affected individuals is often not taken seriously, and I was constantly told that I was 'just a bit bendy' or that I was experiencing growing pains or hormonal changes. I knew from a young age that something more was happening compared to my peers, but many doctors did not see this.

As I got older and began to advocate for myself more, it was clear that some doctors did not like the fact I was able to do so. I was told that I couldn't have a condition if I was managing to go to school (which I was only just about managing to do).

At age 17, a senior cardiologist told me that I just had 'naughty girl syndrome' – it couldn't be that I was experiencing dysautonomia, but instead that I was simply not drinking enough water. He hadn't even taken my whole appointment – the junior doctor who saw me only wanted to check whether his intended referral plans would be sufficient. He sent me away and told me to drink more, but the next senior cardiologist I saw diagnosed me with POTS almost instantly.

There is not only bias in individual doctors, though. This is a systemic issue affecting people every single day, and is one which is also clear when it comes to neurodivergence and autism, as we will explore in this chapter. I have little doubt that I would have been diagnosed autistic years earlier if I was a white boy, which could have prevented much of the crisis and trauma I went through as a teenager.

Alongside this, we will hear from a range of chronically ill autistic people with intersectional experiences who are multiply marginalised in such settings, such as being Black, from the Global South, or being trans and non-binary. It is crucial to understand how being multiply marginalised provides additional challenges, and to explore the privileges many of us can hold simultaneous to being marginalised in some ways.

Medical misogyny and autism

No-one even uttered the word autism about me until I started to fall into mental health crisis and had panic attacks, but when I look back at my childhood, it is extremely obvious. Knowing so much now about everything from interoception to not gelling with girls my own age and preferring to be around teachers, to the reason why I've walked on my toes since I was three years old – it's crystal clear.

Some might just say that that's the nature of hindsight – but there's far more to it than that. Society still sees autism as a white boy condition, compounded by both the medical system and the media. The red flags in boys were, in me, simply seen as being a shy and quirky girl.

The idea that autism can only occur in boys is a long-standing one, one which as a community we are still having to fight every day. Autism Speaks perpetuated this for years through their use of the colour blue and use of images only of boys, for example. You don't have to look hard for individuals who have thought this their whole life, even now – I encounter people almost every week who don't understand how I could be autistic.

Whilst I was diagnosed due to mental health crisis and an ortho-paedic doctor eventually seeing a red flag in my toe-walking, many go undiagnosed until they are multiple decades into life. It is not uncommon for them to be diagnosed at 30, 40, if at all.

There is no 'female autism' or specific autism that is found in women, girls or those assigned female at birth. Many have mis-conceptions about this, and there is a rapidly increasing misun-derstanding that there are different autisms found in different genders. Although some traits may present subtly differently, causing them to be missed by many parents, teachers and doc-tors alike, and masking may be more common in those assigned female at birth, this does not mean there is a separate brain wiring.

We talk more about masking in Chapter 9. There are plenty of autistic people assigned male at birth who are also a 'masked Autistic' (as coined by Dr Devon Price) and experience significant masking, to the extent I know some who have been told they have a 'female brain' by medical professionals. This is tied closely to medical misogyny as they demonstrate the assumption that these traits are associated with meekness or quirkiness, for example. That said, it seems that those assigned female at birth are more likely to mask, possibly due to the way we are socialised around specific gender roles, whether that be accidentally or purposefully – such as being more open to eye contact, being quieter, not drawing attention to ourselves or focusing on housework or academic work compared to practical.

The diagnostic criteria for autism are inherently misogynistic and sexist, focused on the way that traits are more likely to manifest in boys (and particularly in those who are very young). For example, a girl lining up her dolls is not seen in the same way as a boy lining up his trains, even though this is from the same autistic trait of pattern recognition and how autistic people play. Similarly, special interests are still often illustrated by an enthusiasm for maths or trains, but should include a broader range, such as gymnastics, books or the colour pink. Some girls who have had special interests in maths or trains are still not picked up because they are just seen as quirky or different.

Diagnosis in those who are misogyny affected is still behind diagnosis in boys. Whilst statistics used to say there could be 16 autistic boys to one autistic girl (using binary gendered language as many studies do), that statistic is falling quickly, and whilst current beliefs seem to argue for four or two to one, it is likely that there is very little difference in the actual numbers, the difference just being in the levels of diagnosis.

The extreme male brain theory played a part in this – Simon Baron-Cohen's theory that men and women are fundamentally different and have different traits, for example empathy being a 'female' trait whilst male brains 'systemise' and recognise patterns instead. He said that autistic people will always have an 'extreme male brain' regardless of sex – contributing to the idea that autism is inherently male, as well as not recognising the differences in the spectrum such as some of us experiencing hyper-empathy rather than a lack of it.

It is clear even in recent years that research around autism still very heavily features cis men and boys over anyone else, studies typically including three to six males for every female.[2] The cycle continues of there not being enough research, so fewer girls are diagnosed, so they are not featured in research.

It is this that also leads to the high rate of misdiagnosis of personality disorders in autistic people assigned female at birth, a combination of autistic people being so likely to be traumatised alongside misconceptions and stereotypes around autism. Whilst there are autistic people who have both autism and emotionally unstable personality disorder, many find themselves misdiagnosed instead. Similarly, we are very likely to be told we just have anxiety and depression, are hysterical or that it's just in our heads, and that we'll get over it. Autism never seems to be the first port of call, because of these stereotypes and misconceptions.

All of this means that many don't find out they are autistic until later in life, and/or after a mental health crisis. It can be difficult to be taken seriously.

One of the things I often advise people who think they are autistic to do is make a list of traits and how these have applied to you – if you are older, this should include both childhood and the present, as much of the assessment will be asking if this has been a constant. Tying your experiences to traits can help some to close the gap between the stereotype and your experience, for example, a special interest of makeup, dolls, music, cooking rather than the stereotypical trains or maths (though you may well have those, and there would be nothing wrong with that either).

Medical misogyny and chronic illness

We know that there is deep medical misogyny when it comes to chronic illnesses. Medical trauma amongst our community is horrifically significant, and it takes many years to decades to be believed or receive a diagnosis.

How many times have you been told that your symptoms are just growing pains, or a product of your periods? To be told that you're simply not looking after yourself, or you can't possibly know what is going on with your body?

This is not only an issue of chronic illness – women are neglected across all aspects of medical care, for example in the way they are represented less in clinical trials, not allowing us to see the impact of drugs on non-male bodies. Similarly, there have been five times as many studies about erectile dysfunction than on premenstrual syndrome, even though 90 percent of women report symptoms of the latter compared to 19 percent of men reporting the former.[3]

However, the issue is naturally faced consistently by those who are assigned female at birth and are seeking a reason for chronic symptoms, a process which often takes years and swathes of doctors.

Some studies show that women are more likely to have more severe levels of pain, pain of longer duration and more frequent pain, and might be more at risk for disabilities related to pain.[4] Others have found that psychological treatments are more likely to be prescribed to female patients, who in addition are more likely to wait longer for or not receive pain medications.[5] These facts combined show a grim reality many of us face – having sometimes worse symptoms, with less support.

It takes an average of eight years to be diagnosed with endometriosis in the UK,[6] despite it affecting at least 10 percent of people with wombs. Many are told that their symptoms are totally normal, despite it being evident that this isn't the case.

Similarly, POTS is a condition which appears to most commonly impact those assigned female at birth, up to 85 percent of patients being so, and between the ages of 13 and 50.[7] Teenage girls and young adults face an intertwining ageism here, and face significant misogyny in medical spaces for 'not drinking enough' or it being put down to only anxiety or panic attacks before doctors will consider even referring them for tests.

In 2020, Angum et al. discussed the prevalence of autoimmune disorders in women through their narrative review, revealing that autoimmune diseases have a gender bias, occurring at a rate of two to one, as well as menstrual and hormonal changes impacting how they affect individuals.[8] Lupus has a huge nine to one ratio. For some autoimmune conditions, women of colour are also more likely to experience them, such as in the case of lupus where African-American women are three times more likely to get lupus than white women.[9] In another study of over 800 women with lupus in the United States, it took participants an average of 3.5 years to be diagnosed, with over 60 percent of them also being misdiagnosed before being diagnosed formally with lupus.[10] Even knowing all of this, it can be significantly difficult for women to be believed, with many misdiagnosed or told not to worry.

Although there are not huge swathes of literature out there explicitly using the term 'medical misogyny' or exploring it when it comes to chronic illness, as a phenomenon it is becoming more and more recognised over time. Healy coined 'Yentl syndrome' to refer to the treatment and underdiagnosis of women,[11] specifically around coronary artery disease, but the idea rings true to many conditions – Yentl was a woman in a short story by Isaac Bashevis Singer who disguised herself as a man. Healy says that women have to pay the price of being like a man in order to experience any semblance of equality or support, and this is true particularly in healthcare.

Medical gaslighting is not exclusive to those who experience medical misogyny, but it can be more common due to its links with misogyny and with misogyny-affected individuals being less likely to be believed – this is also much worse for other marginalised groups such as Black or Asian individuals, meaning of course that Black and Asian women experience dual discrimination in this sense. This refers to when healthcare concerns are dismissed or minimised to the point you question your own reality. Sometimes this can be difficult to spot, but if you are being constantly told your symptoms are just weight or anxiety related, this might be occurring, or if they tell you what you're experiencing is totally normal or not considered problematic.

This can make life extremely difficult to live – living in pain or having other symptoms whilst being constantly told there is nothing wrong and that our normal test results are a good thing have significant mental impact and can make us often likely to experience emotional dysregulation, suicidality and anxiety.

What I want you to know is that if you experience chronic pain, fatigue or any other symptoms from excess thirst to gastrointestinal issues – you are valid, and deserve to have answers found for you. You are not hysterical, nor an attention seeker.

In Dec 2019–Feb 2020, I was in a really extremely painful experience related to my colitis, that didn't present classically as colitis. I saw three doctors who dismissed my pain (all male) because it didn't make sense with my diagnosis, and then prescribed me meds that actually made the situation WORSE because of their poor diagnosis. The last one literally used the word hysterical and I almost laughed out loud, except that I was in too much pain. Finally I saw a woman GP who just... believed me, and found me a women gastroenterologist who ALSO believed me, and I was being treated properly within days. – **Emily**

The combination of chronic illness, autism and misogyny

Whilst people who are either autistic or chronically ill will often experience medical misogyny, there is also a unique presentation of this found in having both conditions.

I have been gaslit by doctors telling me I can't possibly know what I am experiencing physically because I'm autistic. Whilst I can struggle to find the right words for my experiences, I know there is something happening – but I have been told I am just an anxious girl and it is all in my head.

The links made between professionals that my neurodivergent brain and my physical symptoms in combination with my gender – because they see misogyny-affected individuals as hysterical or fussing for nothing – is misogynist and ableist in a deeply harmful combination.

Part of my autistic self is my special interests and ability to deeply focus on a topic – there is a clear reason why I would end up researching and focusing on the chronic symptoms that were impacting every single second of my life and were being seen as something normal by some doctors and as a mystery by others. Being judged by doctors for knowing 'too much' is a product of ableism towards autistics, and seeing female-presenting patients as hysterical is a product of sexism.

One study discusses estimations of pain from non-verbal cues and how this is used within assumptions by professionals about whether the patient is believed. Overall, women are perceived to be in less pain than men even if they rate their pain to be the same level.[12] As an autistic and female-presenting individual, the reliance on non-verbal cues by professionals is dangerous because I do not present non-verbally in the same way as others might.

When women and those who are assigned female at birth are assumed to be hysterical, it is no wonder why those who are autistic and struggle to communicate in words the format of their symptoms are not believed, because the assumption is that if you are experiencing something you should be able to tap into your body and understand and describe it. Our interoception often means we cannot do this, and in trying to find the words, we are often seen as stalling or making it up on the spot.

My sensory needs also mean that I often struggle with tests or being touched by doctors, particularly if this is without warning like it often is when you first go to someone in primary care, meaning they are sometimes more likely to be inclined to believe that I am exaggerating or not telling the truth.

Knowing that autism can be co-occurring with many other conditions and chronic illnesses, it is likely no surprise that endometriosis and PCOS are becoming increasingly researched as co-occurring conditions for autistic people with uteruses. We also seem to disproportionately experience pre-menstrual dysphoric disorder (PMDD), and heavier or more painful periods. However, knowing that those who experience any of these conditions are often fobbed off and told their periods or period symptoms are totally normal, we can also see how autistic people with periods who are less able to specifically identify such symptoms due to interoception might be less likely to receive support for these conditions. We will discuss these conditions more later in this chapter.

With the knowledge that POTS and EDS both co-occur with autism, and both disproportionately impact those assigned female at birth, this is a very common diagnostic cluster. But, rather than this being recognised and looked for, we are told that we can't have that many conditions, or we are diagnosis shopping, making up symptoms or experiencing them only in relation to our original diagnosis. I often say that it feels like once you get tested for one, you should be referred for testing for them all.

Alice is a disabled and neurodivergent young woman. She said:

> I've been told I'm making it up and it's all in my head, which seems to happen more with girls and women. The element of not being believed is something I've experienced a lot. It's a very conflicting experience to have so many symptoms and traits happening at the same time and your identity being brought into it.
>
> Being chronically ill and neurodivergent affects me as a woman in that I never experience the key events that others do. For example, I have no interest in going to parties, but it's something I can't really do. – **Alice**

I'm a doctor or healthcare professional – how do I stop this from occurring?

Firstly, even being aware of medical misogyny and these gaps is probably going to start mental processes that you might not have had before. But, the next step is to put that into practice and work to make things better. Here are some pointers for how you might begin to do so:

- Learn more about chronic illnesses and those which are more likely to affect those assigned female at birth. Consider the symptoms you might assume are anxiety or something else, and think about how you can make sure you are hearing people properly.

- Learn more about conditions which are commonly co-occurring. Many have to go back through processes for years even though many of their conditions should have been picked up at a similar time due to what they were expressing.

- Don't rely on non-verbal communication or on hearing what you perceive as the 'right' words for different types of pain or symptoms in order to believe them.

- Consider if you would be saying the same thing to someone male-presenting who had the same symptoms.

- Unlearn stereotypes and misogynistic ideas you might have been taught or picked up throughout your career. You could do this through discussion with misogyny-affected colleagues, keeping up to date on new research around medical misogyny, reading articles and books from individuals with lived experience, and being self-reflective on your practice.

- Make sure you are talking people through any testing or procedures required, as well as through your thought processes on why (or why not) you are referring them to someone else. Document this and challenge if it does not happen.

Advocating for yourself around medical misogyny

There is not really a specific way to advocate for yourself around medical misogyny as compared to advocating for yourself on a general level as an autistic and chronically ill individual. It can also be the case that you may not feel safe to stand up against it for fear of making a serious accusation that will be seen as inflammatory or offensive, particularly if you attend appointments alone. It might make you anxious that you won't get the tests or referrals that you need.

A way that you can self-advocate is by pre-empting this sort of response. Have a diary of your experiences ready or a list of what you are experiencing (in the case of an autism or neurodivergent diagnosis, where these have occurred in childhood is also significantly useful as they will be wanting to know this at some point anyway).

You might also find it helpful to make notes or write down any questions you have as you go. This can make some doctors less likely to make throwaway comments and can make you much more able to follow up on any concerns. I find myself very scrambled in appointments due to the pace of them, the masking I am doing and the issues of the sensory and social environment, so I often don't remember to ask questions until afterwards.

Remember that you are allowed to ask to see someone else. It is within your rights as a patient to see someone else if you are uncomfortable or feel you are experiencing an issue like medical misogyny or gaslighting. It is not always this simple, as there might be longer wait times to see another person, or there might not be another specialist in your condition – but it is an avenue worth exploring if possible. If you feel comfortable, you might want to put in a formal complaint in some situations. Many hospitals will have patient liaison services that can support you with this or take them forward for you.

As discussed in Chapter 1 about attending appointments, it can be helpful to have someone with you who can reinforce that you are not just experiencing anxiety or that it isn't a new concern, or whatever reason the doctor might use for not addressing your concerns. Obviously, it can be a privilege to have someone available to go with you – but it can be helpful as back-up particularly if you are having recurring issues.

Remember that no-one knows you better than you know yourself. As autistic and chronically ill people, feeling like we know our bodies isn't always the easiest thing – but no-one else knows it better than you do. Good professionals will listen to the way we talk about our bodies and work with you to understand what that means in a medical context, and won't gaslight you into thinking you've made it up.

Menstrual health conditions

We discussed periods when it comes to sensory needs in Chapter 3, but many autistic people will also be dealing with chronic illnesses related to their menstrual health systems such as endometriosis, PCOS and PMDD.

These conditions can mean difficulties with the menstrual cycle such as it being irregular, which can be difficult for autistic people due to struggling with changes or a lack of routine – not knowing when you might have a period, for example. Periods might also be heavier, making sensory needs more difficult to cope with.

Like with other chronic illnesses, difficulties with interoception as an autistic person can make it harder to process symptoms or mean you are hypersensitive or hyposensitive to them. You might also struggle with emotional dysregulation and find this worsens at points in your cycle, making you feel depressed, anxious or suicidal.

It can be helpful to use an app such as Clue to track your menstrual health, particularly if you are forgetful or are wanting to spot any patterns. On many of them, you can track different elements such as pain, emotion, sleep, sexual activity or skin, alongside your period itself.

It is estimated that 5 to 10 percent of women and individuals assigned female at birth of reproductive age have PMDD, though this doesn't account for misdiagnosis or those missed, as well as those whose cycle is suppressed.[13]

Neve has PCOS and PMDD. She talked about the impact of her PMDD:

PMDD has eaten over a decade of my life. In my early child-hood, I went through all the usual trauma that undiagnosed autistic people can, like bullying, but I was still able to be happy. My periods started at 12 and when I hit 14 all the hap-piness drained out of my life. I attributed it to my abuse at school and home. I was diagnosed autistic at 23 and thought I would get proper support, which didn't happen.

A year or so later uncontrollable week-long panic attacks started. They became more regular until I found I was having them once a month. I told my GP I thought they were con-trolled by hormones and he referred me to a gynaecologist.

Having severe PMDD means I can barely hold my life together – if it's not damage, it's damage recovery. I have monthly injections to induce chemical menopause, which stops my periods and therefore my PMDD for six-, nine- or 12-month blocks. Unfortunately, due to concerns about bone health, it was recommended I have three-month breaks. My period and PMDD would come back on month two of the break and wouldn't stop until injection number three. So just as I would be getting back on my feet again with chemical menopause, I would have to take the break and go back to square one. Now I'm on indefinite chemical menopause until I can have surgically induced menopause.

I'm a self-taught 2D/3D artist and animator so I spend my

> time at home practicing when I feel well enough. I've been in a few exhibitions but it's the PMDD and lack of social skills that's held me back from making a career out of it. – **Neve**

PMDD, like autism, is often misdiagnosed as borderline personality disorder or bipolar disorder. Neve recommends that if you menstruate and feel like your moods get out of control once every month, you should consider the possibility of PMDD.

Track your periods and moods, and you may find there is a part of your cycle where this occurs. These are often at the luteal phase but not always.

Endometriosis is also a common menstrual health condition, where tissue grows in places outside of the womb lining.

My mum, Awen, has a recent diagnosis of endometriosis, and learnt she was autistic at the age of 36, when I was diagnosed. She told me about the discovery of being a chronically ill autistic person:

> I had just turned 40 when the pain started. I had been having pain at ovulation for a long time, but this one month the pain just didn't stop. I did the sensible thing and went to the GP and a few months, an ultrasound and a painful gynaecological exam later I was diagnosed with endometriosis. It was all a bit of a whirlwind and I remember the consultant being very confused when I didn't just accept the treatment he was offering me or why I was crying about what he called a 'good diagnosis'. At this point it had been a few years since I had come to realise that I was almost certainly autistic, following the diagnosis of my two older children. It made so much sense of my earlier life and struggles then and since. What didn't

occur to me until fairly recently was the impact being autistic would have on dealing with a physical health problem.

I am a deeply rejection sensitive autistic and it is completely normal to me to put everyone else first. As a mum of four and a wife and trying to run a business, all of that is far more important than me or anything I might be dealing with. So as a result I often just push through, even on days when the pain is bad, frequently forgetting to even take pain relief.

One particularly bad day when I must have been complaining about the pain and how bad I was feeling, my eldest very pointedly said 'endometriosis is a chronic illness you know, it does count'. To be honest, I think I thought it would eventually just go away, that I would get better because that was the logical conclusion. It's been a lot to accept that it might not. – **Awen**

Being trans or non-binary as an autistic and chronically ill individual

I came out as non-binary in 2022. I started having more intense thoughts that I might be in 2021, although I'd wondered previously. It was really no surprise to my family, considering I've always felt detached from 'womanhood', my periods and childbirth, and I also legally changed my name to my gender-neutral nickname when I was 17. Whilst you can do all of those things and be a cis woman, it turned out that I certainly wasn't. Statistics say that autistic individuals are around three to six times more likely to be non-binary, transgender or gender non-conforming than their allistic peers[14] – and this makes a lot of sense when you consider the nature of gender as a social construct.

What this does mean is facing another aspect of marginalisation as a chronically ill autistic, in a number of ways including within healthcare, mental health care and society at large.

If you have a uterus and are trans or non-binary, this can cause significant levels of gender dysphoria within yourself which can then be compounded by chronic menstrual conditions, having painful periods or being constantly told you are a female when accessing healthcare.

Non-binary people are not recognised at a governmental level, and there are lots of doctors who are still not at a point of understanding and respecting those who are trans or non-binary during appointments, so these can often be distressing spaces to enter – and spaces we are entering disproportionately often as chronically ill individuals.

There are, of course, ways to affirm yourself at the beginning of appointments – you can talk about your pronouns or discuss your gender and they can respect it. But, for many that is a simple thing to do and does not always feel safe, so misgendering and feeling unsafe can cause more dysphoria.

If you do choose to disclose this, professionals must keep this confidential. You also have the right to have your name and gender changed on medical records whether or not you have or intend to have a Gender Recognition Certificate.

If you do want to get a referral to a gender identity clinic, some autistic and chronically ill individuals have faced difficulties due to their conditions, like Eli.

Eli is transmasculine. He said:

Not long after I came out, I went to talk to my GP about it. They presumed it was just a 'special interest' and didn't refer me for further support. Years later, I got the confidence to go again and did get a referral to the Gender Identity Clinic.

During my screening appointment, they were very concerned about how being autistic, my mental health and my physical health would impact on my transition. I've not heard anything back since. I'm worried that these will continue to be barriers for me.

I've found a lot of people with similar experiences and intersectional identities to mine within the queer community. It has been a source of strength, despite feeling the impact of rising transphobia. The stigma has been stressful and impacted my health, but the community is really a source of healing. – **Eli**

Jasper is a transgender man. He talked about the difference his transition has made as a chronically ill and autistic person:

There were positives and negatives to the effects on my body when I started hormones. EDS is linked to collagen, so women or those assigned female at birth are more prone to dislocations and other risks, as there isn't as much strength, whereas for people who have more testosterone this is less of a problem. The frequency of dislocations reduced, although it is still an issue. The stereotype of EDS is a soft, young face and the texture of my skin is very different to how it was before. When you first start hormones your behaviour and aggression can be very different and cause added stress, which isn't great for the body when you have EDS.

Most of the community is cishet women, and EDS is more known to affect women. Things that are said can be quite transphobic or cisnormative, so I can't get involved in conversations without having to awkwardly ask if they don't say that and having to come out as trans to a stranger on the internet. Some spaces are really transphobic too. – **Jasper**

Dylan told me about being non-binary, masking and having a condition that caused early menopause.

I navigated early menopause due to premature ovarian failure in my 20s without knowing I was autistic and how autism impacts the menopausal experience, and while being non-binary. This was a profoundly isolating experience, especially given the intense dysphoria that accompanies hormonal depression. I feel uncomfortable with how gendered my medical experiences are, from overly feminine graphics on pamphlets to nurses calling me 'girl' (I am not typically out to my medical providers). HRT absolutely impacts my symptoms, as low estrogen contributes to executive dysfunction, and I'm still in the process of tweaking my doses and delivery methods.

I'm AFAB, but 'female' felt like a club I never really belonged in, a feeling familiar to neurodivergent people. There are so many parallels between realising I was non-binary and realising I was autistic. I notice that when I mask my autism, it often involves masking my gender; I pitch my naturally deep voice up on work calls, for instance. The same vague sense of, 'What memo did everyone but me get?' that I feel when interacting with neurotypical people generally I also felt when interacting with cis women. I've been told by bosses that my direct communication style would be fine for a man, but unbecoming for a woman. – **Dylan**

MS lives in Indonesia and talked about how being non-binary, autistic and chronically ill all interact together.

Being non-binary, and chronically ill and autistic makes so much sense to me and it increases my chances to learn about myself even more. It reduces my anxiety about a lot of things that I didn't know have connections. Like gender expression and being neurodivergent. But it does affect social life and functions. Being non-binary is still very taboo in the place where I live, especially when I'm visually presenting (visually and physically obvious that I don't follow stereotypical gender norms). I got misjudged and misunderstood a lot.

I am mainly a masculine presenting non-binary in most of my days. To the norm, I'm expected to be strong, high stamina, quick, and rough. But as a chronically ill person, there are limitations to my physique... Most people don't believe me and often I found myself in trouble for pushing beyond my physical limitations. – **MS**

Dan is a 24-year-old non-binary person. They are AuDHD (autistic with ADHD) and have fibromyalgia and ME. They said:

I know that because many people believe my appearance doesn't match my pronouns, as I have not undertaken medical transition nor have I done much to change my appearance to look more androgynous or masculine, I simply would not be taken seriously by many medical professionals, something that happens often enough as it is. I know that this would also invite a lot of questions and distract from the goal of obtaining the healthcare I need and am asking for. Many of my trans friends get invasive questions about their gender, transition status, genitals, and so on, when they are trying to access healthcare unrelated to any of that. Frankly, I get stressed and anxious enough about trying to advocate for my own health and autonomy without the addition of transphobia, so I've decided not to engage with medical professionals about that part of my identity. – **Dan**

For more general information about being transgender or non-binary and autistic, I recommend *Queerly Autistic* by Erin Ekins (2021).

KEY TAKEAWAYS FROM THIS CHAPTER

- Experiences of medical gaslighting and medical misogyny do happen and are not your fault.
- Diagnosis can be much tougher for marginalised people, and this is part of why self-diagnosis is seen as valid in the autistic and disabled communities.
- Sometimes autism and chronic illness can intertwine to impact your experience of medical misogyny.
- Transmisogyny can also occur in medical settings.
- Trans and non-binary people have rights within healthcare regardless of transition or having a Gender Recognition Certificate.

9

Disability pride and disability joy

A lot of this book has been all about some of the truly difficult parts of being a chronically ill and autistic person in a society made for non-disabled people, and whilst we need to discuss all of that, I want to leave you with a chapter all about the great parts of being who we are and how you can begin to lean into your identities and love yourself.

It has taken me a long time to embrace being disabled, but I honestly do love my disabled self, and more than anything, I absolutely love my community.

Loving yourself

Within society, we are told disability is not a good thing. We're scrounging off the system or being difficult when we ask for accommodations. Most of us will be told at some point that we're faking.

When it is seen as a good thing, it's often in the context of inspiration porn – which refers to when disability is used to make non-disabled people feel better about themselves or to inspire them to 'do better', because they believe that if a disabled person can do something, they do not have an excuse.

In a society with these views, one that doesn't want us to be happy about being disabled and wants us to defy our conditions, it can be extremely difficult to find self-love and to figure out who we truly are.

Autistic masking

When you are autistic, there's an added level to loving yourself and being yourself – our ability to, and often unconscious effort to, mask. Masking is also sometimes called 'social camouflaging', and refers to when autistic people emulate being an allistic person in an effort to survive in a neurotypical society.

This is not something that is simple to unlearn, as it is often extremely layered. You might find you are able to more easily unmask more outward behaviours like not forcing yourself to make eye contact when you don't want to, but find it much harder to unmask the ways that you dress or stim in public, for example.

An extremely good resource on unmasking is *Unmasking Autism* by Dr Devon Price (2022), which I would recommend if you want to begin to focus on this more heavily. Price discusses the ways that society is responsible for helping autistic people unmask, with it not only being an individual effort, and he also discusses the privileges behind being able to unmask.

For many of us, it is unlikely we will ever be completely unmasked for a variety of reasons. Society's expectations often mean that it often feels needed, and there are so many layers to it that we may never know the total sum of our masks. It is not a simple thing to do, and can take years – I personally don't think I'll ever become totally unmasked.

As a chronically ill person, your symptoms may impact your autistic masking. For example, you may also be dealing with trying not to show that you are in pain or fatigued, and this might combine with you masking how you communicate. Alternatively, it could mean your autistic masking lessens due to lack of energy or putting your focus elsewhere.

There are a lot of different ways that individuals might both unmask or more generally help themselves feel more self-love as a disabled person. Some of these will be more surface-level changes, such as those to your aesthetic, whereas others will be more internal.

Here are some of the ways I have found self-love and begun to unmask:

- Wearing clothing that is comfortable, sensory friendly and is patterned or brightly coloured instead of clothing that I feel like I should wear. For me this includes dungarees, soft fleeces, puffer jackets, bralettes and jumpsuits.
- Using disability aids that aren't just grey or standardised – I have previously had purple walking sticks and I've been known to wrap them in fairy lights!
- Using badges, stickers and lanyards to notify the public that I am disabled to a level that I am comfortable with, and not making myself answer questions from strangers with more detail than I want to.
- Finding ways to use makeup that express myself, and not wearing it just because society wants me to – I find foundation and heavy base products give me sensory overload and are difficult to apply, but I love wearing glittery eyeshadows and highlighters.
- Becoming more confident to stim in public – this can be very difficult, but over time I have learnt which stim toys or movements I am comfortable with in public, meaning I can regulate myself. It is worth noting that for some marginalised communities this can be more dangerous, so this is also a privileged way of finding my self-love and unmasking.

- Taking pictures with my disability aids – I used to hate looking at photos of myself and would refuse to be in photos with my family, and when I first got a walking stick I wouldn't let it feature. Over time, I began to take more photos and become comfortable with showing the world my disabilities. Now, my Instagram photos are rarely without them if I'm using them at the time.
- Exploring my identities and who I am in therapy and going to physiotherapy and doing exercise as a way to support myself, not to try and fix myself.
- Trying to communicate in the ways that support me and come naturally rather than the ways others do, and not forcing eye contact so often.
- Using alternative forms of communication like typing on my phone or using the 'Big' app, rather than forcing myself to speak.

These are only a few of the things that have helped me. You may find other things empowering – a couple of other examples might be getting involved in different hobbies, making artwork or playing with different hairstyles. You might also find that joining groups that help you interact with other disabled people or people with your condition might empower you and make you feel like you belong. Every disabled person will find different things that provide self-love.

Of course, all of these things take time. Don't put pressure on yourself to become confident and full of self-love overnight – it has taken me a decade of getting used to my conditions, learning about my body, and beginning to work out how I need to unmask. But, I promise that it is not impossible, and you *deserve* to feel good about yourself.

I think the process of unmasking as an autistic person has been transformative for how I treat myself, and think of myself, as a person with colitis and chronic pain. I didn't identify as a disabled person until so recently. When I was highly masked, I expected 150 percent of myself all the time – physically, mentally, emotionally. I ignored SO MUCH about my own needs, and I wanted to be a 'normal person', so I thought that meant being someone who could eat what everyone ate, go to parties that everyone went to, etc. And now I am learning a much softer way to think of my own life, and it's coming from the autism work but it's also meaning that I am more open with myself, and with other people, about my physical needs as well – I need to go to a park that has a public bathroom; sometimes I can't do an overnight visit; I'll bring my own food/drink to something; etc. – **Emily**

It is also important to say that disability does not have to be positive or negative. Often we see non-disabled people saying our conditions are not disabilities, but instead they are superpowers, or that we should focus on 'ability first'. This implies the word 'disability' to be negative, when to many of us it is positive or simply neutral in tone. I love who I am, I love being disabled – but I also have times where I wish for something different. It's not the same in every moment, or for every condition, or every person.

You can also have different feelings about your different conditions. I have much heavier, harder to process feelings about my chronic illnesses compared to being autistic and neurodivergent. I would give the former up if I could, whereas I don't have that sort of feeling about my neurodivergence. Ultimately, however, each and every part of being disabled is who I am, and I still see it as a neutral part of life and society. Those feelings then tie into disability pride.

Disability pride

You will find a strong sense from many disabled people that they are proud of their identity as well as being proud to be part of a community.

They might be proud to be disabled for different reasons – it might be due to the strength they feel they have, loving the community, or standing strong against ableism and inaccessibility within society.

It is important to say that you can be proud to be disabled and still have days where you wish things were different, whether that be because you don't want to be in pain anymore, or you want to be able to go out with your friends more easily, or you're tired of people not giving you the support you need.

Some days I'd like to climb out of my own body for a few hours. Get away from pain, fatigue, the overwhelm fireworks or chewing noises give me. Being disabled can be extremely difficult, and we are allowed to acknowledge the ways it is and how it impacts each day.

But I'm still so proud to be disabled. I adore being around people who totally understand me. I love my ability to hyperfocus, the way I can learn so much about specific topics, and I adore stimming; spinning around, using tangle toys, or watching coloured LED lights. I love the way it makes me want to consume so much knowledge, and how it makes me question why society is the way it is so often.

I'm also so proud of every way I stand against a society that is so heavily built on ableism, that wants me to hate my conditions or hide them.

This is often confusing to some non-disabled people – why would we be proud of it when disability is often seen as not the norm, as not right?

That's because non-disabled people see disability as a deficit, meaning they believe it is a fault. To many of us, it should instead just be seen as a form of diversity. We are not less than our non-disabled peers.

I asked our contributors to tell me why they are proud to be disabled:

Being disabled isn't a bad thing – every single person is an individual and has a lot to give, both to the world and to the disabled community. I've found friends for life because of my conditions and I'm incredibly proud of them. I feel like I can educate people on being a young person with chronic illness and disabilities and I find it really empowering to show people that disabled people aren't just the stereotype; we're not all in wheelchairs, we don't all have the same access needs. I've been in the disabled community for over 20 years and I feel like it is my home. – **Meg**

Being disabled is always the first thing I say about myself. This is my identity and it's very important to me because it's been pivotal to my life. I grew up with my mum taking me to disabled children's groups and it's always been a part of who I am – if you try to take the disability out there wouldn't be anything, there would just be a hole. It's given me access to my friends, my work, my degree and my partner. It's a very positive thing for me. – **Jasper**

I think it makes me more accepting and empathic. I know how it feels to be discriminated against and looked down upon, so I try to stand up for others. – **JJ**

I'm proud because of all the things I have learnt. I am a lot more open minded since becoming disabled and see the beauty in the small things. If I never got ill, I think I would be more ableist and seek my value in the things I get done. I'm proud of the world view I have now and the person I have become. I'm also proud of the disability community, especially on Instagram. They have taught me to be kind to my body and better listen to it. That 'pushing through' isn't a good idea most of the time when you have a chronic illness. This is also important, because a lot of my emotions I don't feel in my head, but through symptoms in my body, like acid reflux for example. Because of the online community I have become more aware of my emotions. – **Marjie**

For me, being autistic means that I am very passionate about my interests, and one of my interests being activism and making change means that I am extremely passionate about it and just won't stop. Autism also means I can read people really well, which a lot of people might associate the opposite with being autistic, but I'm very perceptive and like to make sure people are ok. Being chronically ill makes me very creative, because it means I find alternative ways of doing things. Because I've also had to drastically change my career path and other things being newly chronically ill, it means instead of focusing on more memory-based subjects like physics, I've actually become more creative recently because it is now easier for me. – **Lauren**

A year ago, I would have said that I was proud of all I have achieved in spite of being disabled, because I appreciate how much harder it is for me to achieve certain things than others. I have come to view this as unhealthy, though, because it tied my value only to my achievements and labelled my disability as a hindrance in the process. Truthfully, there is little I enjoy about having PCOS or dyspraxia, but I am trying to take pride in being autistic as much as possible. I am proud of my enhanced memory, my pattern-spotting abilities, my strong sense of justice and my advanced knowledge of key subjects. Beyond this, I am proud to be disabled in any sense of the word because I am finding great solace in being part of the disability community. I am proud to have common ground and many shared experiences with a range of disabled people I have come to admire, and am glad that such admiration is based on who they are as people rather than their achievements. – **Harriet**

I'm unbelievably proud to be disabled. I think it has allowed me to have great compassion for others and the bravery to point out where structures are a barrier for people.

I'm proud of how far I've come, despite seemingly never-ending obstacles. I'm one hell of a fighter, even when sick and exhausted.

I'm proud of the rest of my community and being a part of that. We have made significant changes to society and have paved the way for future generations to live autonomous lives. – **Eli**

'Proud' is a bit of a strong word for me because I'm very much feeling the 'disabled' part of being disabled right now. What I will say though is that I feel my autism is inextricable from my identity and as such I don't believe there is a 'cure'. I'm proud of how the community has come together as a sort of counterculture to the norm. It's helped me feel a little better about being the black sheep of my family ever since I was little. I also believe my autism is the reason I have been able to improve my artistic and writing talents through self-study. I can only hope I can achieve some kind of success with them someday.

I'm not proud to be disabled by PMDD – not even in the 'what doesn't kill you makes you stronger' sense. It has not made me resilient. – **Neve**

I'm proud of the advocacy and support I provide other disabled people. We rely on one another to make up for our physicians' deficits. I have supported many people through the process of diagnosis and finding treatments and accommodations that work for them. I'm proud of the knowledge I've acquired. I'm proud of what I've accomplished despite ableism trying to hold me back. – **Dylan**

I think being disabled gives me a lot of insights and perspectives that people without disability don't experience. I am basically living in a different reality than most people; I see with different eyes. I feel like this experience humbles me a lot when I was thinking about 'what ifs'. What if I don't have disabilities? I might not be this grounded and wise, I might not be this creative and unique, and I might not see beauty the same as if I don't have disabilities. As a disabled person, I see beauty in things that aren't normally seen as such. And that itself is already a blessing for me.

Disability defines me as an authentic being. And living as me is all that I want. – **MS**

I wouldn't personally use the word 'proud' to be disabled, I'd rather say that I have accepted being disabled and that there is nothing wrong with it. We are all unique, amazing people and we all have different needs and accommodations. What I am proud of though is that I can try to use my voice to help change things, whilst also amplifying the voices of others. – **Adam**

I facilitate workshops a lot (online and in person) and I am proud to be modelling my own accommodations to students. I'm proud to be a disabled teacher and to be open with them about my own needs so that they can be open with theirs. – **Emily**

Disabled people are really cool. I can adapt anything, I know my body doesn't work properly and my brain works differently but I can deal with so many things. It's part of my identity and it's taken me a while to accept but I can work to break down the barriers put up in front of me. I can help break them down for the next generations and there is power in that. As much as it is horrific some days, you have so much power in understanding your body and using it as a force for good. – **Alice**

I am proud to be autistic as it gives me a different look on life, and I believe this helps me come up with new ideas. I also think my chronic illnesses have allowed me to have opportunities that I would not have had without them. – **Becky**

My disability pride also partly comes from the history of the Disability Rights Movement. This includes the work of disabled activists in America who worked towards the Americans with Disabilities Act (ADA) which passed in 1990. As part of the protests for the ADA, there was a famous protest where disabled people got out of their wheelchairs and climbed up the stairs of the Capitol building – as there wasn't a ramp up to the entrance, proving the need for the law to pass. This included Jennifer Keelan-Chaffins, who was only eight years old.[1]

Similarly, in the United Kingdom, disabled activists worked towards the Disability Discrimination Act which passed in 1995.

In 1992, disabled activists marched into the headquarters of Telethon '92, which was a 28-hour fundraiser by ITV which was showing damaging ideas around disability and preying on stereotypes that were unacceptable.[2]

Since the beginning of austerity in the UK in 2010, the Disability Rights Movement has continued to have influence and continued pushing back. The Disabled People Against Cuts (DPAC) group has been a huge part of this work and been a part of both physical protest and online protest.[3] They also protested during the 2012 Paralympic Games against the portrayal of disabled individuals.

The role of disability activism in our history is a huge part of why we can be proud to be disabled, and be proud of our identities and community.

People you can follow online

Autism and/or chronic illness

@littlehux (Twitter)
@commaficionado (Twitter)
@sarahmarieob (Twitter)
@queerlyautistic (Twitter)
@saraheboon (Twitter)
@AnnMemmott (Twitter)
@AutSciPerson (Twitter)
@poppyfield (Twitter and Instagram)
@livedexperienceeducator (Instagram)
@autienelle (Instagram)
@neurodivergent_lou (Instagram)
@iampayingattention (Instagram)
@chloeshayden (Instagram)
@KateStanforth (Instagram)
@lifeofpippa (Instagram)
@neurodiversitywithlozza (Instagram)
@ellen__jones (Instagram)
@yen_godden (Instagram)

@allie_wrote (Instagram)
@youlookokaytome (Instagram)
@ellie_ology (Instagram)
@disabled_eliza (Instagram and TikTok)
@elliemidds (Instagram and TikTok)
@notabadperiod (Instagram)

Disability

@Imani_Barbarin (Twitter)
@Tinu (Twitter)
@keah_maria (Twitter and Instagram)
@crutches_and_spice (Instagram)
@nina_tame (Instagram)
@sophjbutler (Instagram)
@makedaisychains (Instagram)

Other resources

Stim edited by Lizzie Huxley-Jones (2020)
Disability Visibility edited by Alice Wong (2020)
Crippled by Frances Ryan (2020)
Unmasking Autism by Dr Devon Price (2022)
Queer Body Power by Essie Dennis (2022)
University and Chronic Illness: A Survival Guide by Pippa
    Stacey (2020)
The Autism Friendly Cookbook by Lydia Wilkins (2022)
*So, I'm Autistic: An Introduction to Autism for Young Adults
    and Late Teens* by Sarah O'Brien (2023)
The Unwritten, online disability publication – www.
    theunwritten.co.uk
Chronically Brown – https://chronicallybrown.com
(un)masked community – www.weareunmasked.com

KEY TAKEAWAYS FROM THIS CHAPTER

- Unmasking autism is not a simple or fast process. You should never beat yourself up if this is difficult for you, and it is valid if it does not feel like something you are safe to do.

- Disability pride isn't always easy to find, but it can be key to understanding yourself and beginning to love and accept who you are.

- There is a huge community out there waiting to support and love you, who will accept you for who you are.

- Being proud of being disabled doesn't mean you are saying it's always a good thing or that it's easy – it's a recognition of who you are and what makes you, you.

Conclusion

As someone who has grown up autistic and chronically ill, undiagnosed for years and then not understanding why advice for one part of me never worked for me as a whole, writing this book has truly been a cathartic experience. I can only hope that this book has helped you too – whether you are that individual going through something similar to what I did, whether you're a parent going through the system with your child, or if you're someone who works with autistic and chronically ill people.

If you're a chronically ill individual – I want you to remember your worth. You deserve to have the care and support you need, to access any education or work that you want to, and to have loving relationships. It certainly can't all automatically click into place, and I won't pretend that reading this book will even begin to touch the surface of stopping all the difficulties you are facing, because of the society we live in often being stacked up against us. But, what I can hope is that you have learnt ways to self-advocate, to love yourself in the face of it all, and learnt some ways you can adjust your own life to make things more comfortable for you.

If you are a parent – I see you. I see you trying to support your child in a world that doesn't want to support young chronically ill and autistic people. I watched my mum's own desperation to get me the support I needed in a system that constantly told us we didn't need anything, that there wasn't anything they could do, and it is horrendous and heart-breaking to watch. I hope you might have learnt a thing or two about advocacy, about alternative communication and supporting your relationship with your young person. Please, remember to look after yourself, too – advocating for your young person can be exhausting and traumatic.

If you are a teacher or a doctor, I hope you have read this book without feeling attacked or misunderstood. Not every professional will cause trauma or hurt to autistic and chronically ill people; not every professional partakes in misogyny or gaslighting or dismissing issues. But, unfortunately, too many do – and I hope you have learnt something about the ways you can subconsciously or institutionally be a part of these forms of ableism or discrimination, and how you can combat this.

I hope that whoever you are, this book has helped you understand the experiences of autistic and chronically ill people and makes you more confident in living life or supporting someone to do so.

Being autistic and chronically ill is often full of truly conflicting experiences, both within your own body and outside of it. But there are ways you can build your life to cope with them, understand them, work with them. I want you to be able to be yourself, and live life in ways you want to, in the best ways you can.

Chronically ill autistic people aren't failures if they are struggling with their traits or symptoms, if they are struggling to interact with the ableist world we live in. Society and its norms can be extremely hard to navigate, and there's no sugar coating that. Every single one of us has a role in making the world more accessible, more friendly, more supportive for them.

So, my final question to you. What are your three biggest takeaways from this book, and what are you going to do with them?

Thank you so much for reading – I wish you the best of luck.

Glossary

Anterior cruciate ligament (ACL) – a ligament within the knee joint which gives stability to the knee.

Assigned female at birth (AFAB) – an individual who was identified as female at the time of birth, generally based on external genitalia. This does not always align with gender identity.

Assigned male at birth (AMAB) – an individual who was identified as male at the time of birth, generally based on external genitalia. This does not always align with gender identity.

Attention deficit hyperactivity disorder (ADHD) – a neurodivergence or neurodevelopmental condition characterised by differences in attention, hyperactivity and impulsivity, as well as causing traits like forgetfulness, hyperfocus, differences in organisational skill, differences with emotional regulation and rejection sensitivity dysphoria.

Autistic – identity-first language term centring autism, a neurodivergence or neurodevelopmental condition including differences in internal and external sensory processing, socialising and communication, as well as often causing a bottom-up thinking style, special interests and a preference for consistency. Autism is different for everyone and refers to a wide range of traits, but this will be discussed in depth throughout the book.

Autonomous sensory meridian response (ASMR) – a sensation felt by some in response to stimuli (for example, tactile, visual or auditory). Many examples of the stimuli are uploaded online for people to listen to or watch.

Cishet – an individual who is cisgender (someone whose gender identity aligns with their assigned sex) and heterosexual (someone who is attracted to one gender opposite or different to their own).

Cisnormative – ways that society reinforces that to be cisgender is the norm, such as through social and gender norms, or the assumption that everyone is cisgender.

Computerised tomography (CT) – a medical imaging scan which emits x-ray beams at different angles to look at internal systems and structures in the body.

Crohn's disease – a chronic inflammatory bowel disease affecting the digestive tract, characterised by inflammation in the digestive system and a range of symptoms such as abdominal pain, loss of appetite, diarrhoea and fatigue, as well as potential complications like obstructions or ulcers.

Dyspraxic – identity-first language term referring to individuals who have dyspraxia, a neurodivergence or neurodevelopmental condition around coordination and motor skills. Dyspraxia may also be known as developmental coordination disorder (DCD) and is characterised by traits such as struggling with fine motor skills (tying shoelaces or handwriting), gross motor skills (driving or playing sports), spatial awareness or organisation.

Ehlers-Danlos syndrome (EDS) – a group of genetic connective tissue disorders including subtypes such as hypermobile EDS (hEDS), classic EDS (cEDS) and vascular EDS (vEDS), amongst others. Each has its own set of symptoms, but they are generally characterised by issues with collagen and connective tissue which provide structure to many of the body's systems, joints, organs and blood vessels. Other symptoms may include fragile or stretchy skin, easy bruising, chronic pain, joint instability (dislocations or subluxations) and cardiovascular or gastrointestinal issues. Many of those with EDS will experience other chronic illnesses alongside it.

Eye movement desensitisation and reprocessing (EMDR) – a type of therapy that uses bilateral stimulation to help process emotional distress.

Fibromyalgia – a chronic illness characterised by widespread musculoskeletal pain alongside cognitive difficulties such as brain fog, fatigue, sleep disturbances, migraines and heightened sensory sensitivity. It may also cause symptoms like irritable bowel syndrome or muscle stiffness.

Gastroparesis – a chronic gastrointestinal illness characterised by delayed stomach emptying, where the stomach muscles responsible for the moving of food through the digestive system are weakened or do not function. Symptoms can include nausea, bloating, vomiting, pain and food intake often being limited.

Hidradenitis suppurativa (HS) – a chronic inflammatory skin condition characterised by painful nodules, inflamed lesions, abscesses or skin scarring, in areas such as but not limited to the armpits, buttocks and groin.

Hypermobility – refers to increased flexibility in the joints beyond what is expected, where joints are more lax or stretchy and bend beyond typical range. This can be a part of hypermobility spectrum disorder (HSD) or hypermobile Ehlers-Danlos syndrome (hEDS), but many individuals may have some level of hypermobility or joint laxity that does not fall into these conditions. It can be associated with joint pain, joint instability and muscle weakness.

Hypermobility spectrum disorder (HSD) – used to describe a group of conditions characterised by a range of symptoms associated with connective tissue disorders without the individual meeting the diagnostic criteria for hEDS or other specific conditions. Symptoms include but are not limited to joint and musculoskeletal pain, joint instability, dislocations or subluxations, chronic fatigue and gastrointestinal issues. HSD can hugely impact quality of life even without meeting hEDS criteria.

Idiopathic intracranial hypertension (IIH) – a chronic illness characterised by increased pressure in the skull, causing a range of symptoms including headaches/migraines, tinnitus, visual disturbance, pain and nausea.

Magnetic resonance imaging (MRI) – a medical imaging scan that uses magnetic fields to make images of internal body structures such as organs or abnormalities.

Mast cell activation syndrome (MCAS) – a chronic illness characterised by excessive or abnormal activation of the mast cells (immune cells which are part of allergic reactions and release of histamines) causing hypersensitivity triggered by factors such as physical exertion, foods or environment. Such reactions can cause a range of symptoms including but not limited to those which are cardiovascular, neurological, respiratory or skin reactions.

Myalgic encephalomyelitis (ME) – a chronic illness characterised by debilitating fatigue and post-exertional malaise (worsening of symptoms following exertion) and a range of other symptoms including brain fog, widespread pain, migraines and sensory sensitivity. ME is sometimes referred to as chronic fatigue syndrome (CFS), but many believe this does not do justice to the experience of the condition.

Non-24-hour sleep wake disorder – a chronic illness relating to the circadian rhythm, where the sleep cycle is not aligned to the

24 hour day/night cycle, leading to difficulty falling asleep when desired, excess daytime sleepiness or shifting of the sleep cycle over periods of time.

Polycystic ovary syndrome (PCOS) – a chronic illness relating to the hormones affecting individuals with ovaries, characterised by ovarian cysts, irregular/absent menstruation and excessive androgens, as well as symptoms such as excess hair growth, weight gain or fertility issues.

Postural orthostatic tachycardia syndrome (POTS) – a chronic illness that falls under the dysautonomia umbrella, characterised by abnormal increases in heart rate when moving to upright positions, with symptoms such as syncope or pre-syncope (fainting or near-fainting), heat and exercise intolerance, and dizziness.

Pre-menstrual dysphoric disorder (PMDD) – an often debilitating mental health condition related to an individual's menstrual cycle, often causing emotional, behavioural and physical symptoms in a cyclical nature around menstruation.

Transgender – an individual whose gender identity is not aligned with their assigned sex at birth.

Endnotes

Introduction

1   Csecs, J. L. L., Iodice, V., Rae, C. L., Brooke, A., Simmons, R., Quadt, L., Savage, G. K., Dowell, N. G., Prowse, F., Themelis, K., Mathias, C. J., Critchley, H. D., & Eccles, J. A. (2022). Joint hypermobility links neurodivergence to dysautonomia and pain. *Frontiers in Psychiatry, 12*, 786916. https://doi.org/10.3389/fpsyt.2021.786916

Chapter 1

1   Hinchey, S. A., & Jackson, J. L. (2011). A cohort study assessing difficult patient encounters in a walk-in primary care clinic, predictors and outcomes. *Journal of General Internal Medicine, 26*(6), 588–594. https://doi.org/10.1007/s11606-010-1620-6

2   Halverson, C. M. E., Clayton, E. W., Sierra, A. G., & Francomano, C. (2021). Patients with Ehlers-Danlos syndrome on the diagnostic odyssey: Rethinking complexity and difficulty as a hero's journey. *American Journal of Medical Genetics Part C: Seminars in Medical Genetics.* https://doi.org/10.1002/ajmg.c.31935

3   All Party Parliamentary Group on Endometriosis. (2020). *Endometriosis UK.* Accessed 21 April 2023 at www.endometriosis-uk.org/sites/default/files/files/Endometriosis%20APPG%20Report%20Oct%202020.pdf

4   Westergaard, D., Moseley, P., Sørup, F. K. H., Baldi, P., & Brunak, S. (2019). Population-wide analysis of differences in disease progression patterns in men and women. *Nature Communications, 10*(666). https://doi.org/10.1038/s41467-019-08475-9

5   Hoffman, K. M., Trawalter, S., Axt, J. R., & Oliver, M. N. (2016). Racial bias in pain assessment and treatment recommendations, and false beliefs about biological differences between blacks and whites. *Proceedings of the National Academy of Sciences, 113*(16), 4296–4301. https://doi.org/10.1073/pnas.1516047113

6   YoungMinds (2023) *Medications*. Accessed 17 May 2023 at www.youngminds.org.uk/young-person/medications

7   Much of the information in this section comes from: The National Autistic Society. (n.d.). *Good practice guide: Adapting talking therapies for autistic adults and children*. Accessed 21 April 2023 at https://s2.chorus-mk.thirdlight.com/file/24/asD-KIN9as.klK7easFDsalAzTC/NAS-Good-Practice-Guide-A4.pdf

8   You can find a sample 'This Is Me' document at: www.nhs.uk/NHSEngland/keogh-review/Documents/quick-guides/background-docs/24-thisisme.pdf.

Chapter 2

1   Kyriacou, C., Forrester-Jones, R., & Triantafyllopoulou, P. (2021). Clothes, sensory experiences and autism: Is wearing the right fabric important? *Journal of Autism and Developmental Disorders, 53*(4), 1495–1508. doi:10.1007/s10803-021-05140-3

2   Carmassi, C., Palagini, L., Caruso, D., Masci, I., Nobili, L., Vita, A., & Dell'Osso, L. (2019). Systematic review of sleep disturbances and circadian sleep desynchronization in autism spectrum disorder: Toward an integrative model of a self-reinforcing

loop. *Frontiers in Psychiatry, 10*, 366. https://doi.org/10.3389/fpsyt.2019.00366

Chapter 3

1 Abraham, D., Heffron, C., Braley, P., & Drobnjak, L. (2015). *Sensory processing 101: Your free chapter.* Accessed 21 April 2023 at https://sensoryprocessing101.com/wp-content/uploads/2015/09/Sensory-Processing-101-Your-Free-Chapter.pdf

2 Little, L. M., Dean, E., Tomchek, S. D., & Dunn, W. (2016). Classifying sensory profiles of children in the general population. *Child: Care, Health and Development, 43*(1), 81–88. https://doi.org/10.1111/cch.12391

3 Much of the information in this section comes from: National Autistic Society. (n.d.). *Sensory differences.* Accessed 21 April 2023 at www.autism.org.uk/advice-and-guidance/topics/sensory-differences/sensory-differences/all-audiences

4 Much of the information in this section comes from: Autism West Midlands. (2019). *Meltdown and shutdown of autistic people.* Accessed 21 April 2023 at https://autismwestmidlands.org.uk/wp-content/uploads/2019/12/Meltdown_and_Shutdown_Nov_2019.pdf

National Autistic Society. (n.d.). *Meltdowns – a guide for all audiences.* Accessed 21 April 2023 at www.autism.org.uk/advice-and-guidance/topics/behaviour/meltdowns/all-audiences

5 Diabetes UK. (n.d.). *Injecting insulin.* Accessed 21 April 2023 at www.diabetes.org.uk/guide-to-diabetes/managing-your-diabetes/treating-your-diabetes/insulin/injecting

6   Crohn's & Colitis UK. (n.d.). *Living with a stoma*. Accessed 21 April 2023 at https://crohnsandcolitis.org.uk/info-support/information-about-crohns-and-colitis/all-information-about-crohns-and-colitis/surgery-and-complications/living-with-a-stoma

Chapter 4

1   Antcliff, D., Keeley, P., Campbell, M., Woby, S., Keenan, A. M., & McGowan, L. (2018). Activity pacing: Moving beyond taking breaks and slowing down. *Quality of Life Research, 27*(7), 1933–1935. https://doi.org/10.1007/s11136-018-1794-7

2   Miserandino, C. (n.d.). *The spoon theory*. Accessed 21 April 2023 at https://butyoudontlooksick.com/articles/written-by-christine/the-spoon-theory

Chapter 5

1   Scope UK. (n.d.). *Ask for interview adjustments*. Accessed 21 April 2023 at www.scope.org.uk/advice-and-support/ask-for-adjustments-at-interview

2   Much of the information in this section comes from: Scope UK. (n.d.). *Reasonable adjustments at work*. Accessed 21 April 2023 at www.scope.org.uk/advice-and-support/reasonable-adjustments-at-work

Chapter 6

1   Merriam-Webster. (n.d.). Independent. In Merriam-Webster.com dictionary. Accessed 21 April 2023 at www.merriam-webster.com/dictionary/independent

Chapter 7

1   Cambridge Dictionary (2023) Ableism. Accessed 17 May 2023 at https://dictionary.cambridge.org/dictionary/english/ableism

2   All Party Parliamentary Group on Endometriosis. (2020). *Endometriosis UK.* Accessed 21 April 2023 at www.endometriosis-uk.org/sites/default/files/files/Endometriosis%20APPG%20Report%20Oct%202020.pdf

3   Merriam-Webster. (n.d.). Gaslighting. In Merriam-Webster.com dictionary. Accessed 21 April 2023 at www.merriam-webster.com/dictionary/gaslighting

Chapter 8

1   Bailey, P. (1966). Hysteria: The history of a disease. *JAMA Psychiatry, 14*(3), 332–333. doi:10.1001/archpsyc.1966.01730090108024

2   Sohn, E. (2019, 13 March). Righting the gender imbalance in autism studies. *Spectrum News.* Accessed 21 April 2023 at www.spectrumnews.org/features/deep-dive/righting-gender-imbalance-autism-studies

3   ResearchGate. (2016, August 12). Why do we still not know what causes PMS? Accessed 21 April 2023 at www.research-gate.net/blog/why-do-we-still-not-know-what-causes-pms

4   Unruh, A. M. (1996). Gender variations in clinical pain experience. *Pain, 65*(2–3), 123–167. https://doi.org/10.1016/ 0304-3959 (95)00214-6

5   Zhang, L., Losin, E. A. R., Ashar, Y. K., Koban, L., & Wager, T. D. (2021). Gender biases in estimation of others' pain. *The Journal of Pain, 22*(9), 1048–1059. https://doi.org/10.1016/j.jpain.2021.03.001

6   All Party Parliamentary Group on Endometriosis. (2020). *Endometriosis UK*. Accessed 21 April 2023 at www.endometriosis-uk.org/sites/default/files/files/Endometriosis%20APPG%20Report%20Oct%202020.pdf

7   Raj, S. R., & Levine, B. D. (2013, February 7). *Postural tachycardia syndrome (POTS) diagnosis and treatment: Basics and new developments*. American College of Cardiology. Accessed 21 April 2023 at www.acc.org/latest-in-cardiology/articles/2016/01/25/14/01/postural-tachycardia-syndrome-pots-diagnosis-and-treatment-basics-and-new-developments

8   Angum, F., Khan, T., Kaler, J., Siddiqui, L., & Hussain, A. (2020). The prevalence of autoimmune disorders in women: A narrative review. *Cureus, 12*(5), e8094. https://doi.org/10.7759/cureus.8094

9   Fernández, M., Calvo-Alén, J., Alarcón, G. S., Roseman, J. M., Bastian, H. M., Fessler, B. J., McGwin Jr, G., Vilá, L. M., Sanchez, M. L., & Reveille, J. D. (2005). Systemic lupus erythematosus in a multiethnic US cohort (LUMINA): XXI. Disease activity, damage accrual, and vascular events in pre- and postmenopausal women. *Arthritis & Rheumatism, 52*(6), 1655–1664.

10 Al Sawah, S., Daly, R., Foster, S., Naegeli, A., Benjamin, K., Doll, H., Bond, G., Moshkovich, O., & Alarcón, G. (2015). Understanding delay in diagnosis, access to care and satisfaction with care in lupus: Findings from a cross-sectional online survey in the United States. *Annals of the Rheumatic Diseases, 74*, 812.

11 Healy, B. (1991). The yentl syndrome. *New England Journal of Medicine, 325*(4), 274–276.

12 Zhang, L., Losin, E. A. R., Ashar, Y. K., Koban, L., & Wager, T. D. (2021). Gender biases in estimation of others' pain. *The*

Journal of Pain, 22(9), 1048–1059. https://doi.org/10.1016/j.jpain.2021.03.001

13 International Association for Premenstrual Disorders. (n.d.). *Facts & figures.* Accessed 21 April 2023 at https://iapmd.org/facts-and-figures

14 Warrier, V., Greenberg, D. M., Weir, E., Buckingham, C., Smith, P., Lai, M. C., Allison, C., & Baron-Cohen, S. (2020). Elevated rates of autism, other neurodevelopmental and psychiatric diagnoses, and autistic traits in transgender and gender-diverse individuals. *Nature Communications, 11*(1), 3959. https://doi.org/10.1038/s41467-020-17794-1

Chapter 9

1 Little, B. (2020, July 24). *When the 'Capitol Crawl' dramatized the need for Americans with Disabilities Act.* Accessed 21 April 2023 at www.history.com/news/americans-with-disabilities-act-1990-capitol-crawl

2 Ryan, F. (2015, November 4). Celebrating the hidden history of disabled people's fight for civil rights. *The Guardian.* Accessed 21 April 2023 at www.theguardian.com/society/2015/nov/04/disabled-people-fight-equal-rights-exhibition-manchester

3 Humphry, D., Clifford, E., Greene, A., Peters, P., & Walker, K. (2020). Introduction to, and interview with, Disabled People Against Cuts. *City, 24*(1–2), 376–399.